THE MAN OF PRINCIPLE

John and Ada Galsworthy

THE MAN
OF PRINCIPLE

A Biography of John Galsworthy

DUDLEY BARKER

Stein and Day / *Publishers* / New York

First STEIN AND DAY PAPERBACK edition 1970

First published in the United States of America in 1969
   by Stein and Day/*Publishers*

Copyright © Dudley Barker 1963

Library of Congress Catalog Card No. 69-17943

All rights reserved

Printed in the United States of America

Stein and Day/*Publishers*/7 East 48 Street, New York, N. Y. 10017

SBN 8128-1297-2

ACKNOWLEDGMENTS

My thanks are due in the first place to John Galsworthy's nephew Rudolf Sauter, and his wife Viola. These two, who from early in their lives knew John and Ada Galsworthy intimately and in later years shared their home and their travels, have not only placed at my disposal the records I wished to consult but have most generously opened up their memories for me. I am indebted to Mr Sauter also, as Galsworthy's Literary Representative since Mrs Galsworthy's death, for permission to quote from Galsworthy's works and from his and Mrs Galsworthy's letters, and from the letters and notes of Mrs Lilian Sauter. In addition, Mr Sauter and his co-Trustee of the Galsworthy estate, Mr A. J. P. Sellar, have kindly made available some detailed information of the Galsworthy family. Among other people who have given me freely of their time and recollections I must in particular thank Mr Hubert Galsworthy, another nephew of the novelist, and Mrs Wilhelmine Galsworthy, the second wife of the novelist's cousin, Major Arthur Galsworthy.

I am grateful to Messrs J. M. Dent & Sons, the publishers, acting on behalf of the trustees of the Joseph Conrad Estate, for permission to quote from letters written by Joseph Conrad; and to Mr David Garnett for permission to quote from those written by his father, Edward Garnett.

Nobody could write of John Galsworthy without relying heavily on the *Life and Letters* written and compiled by his close friend, the late H. V. Marrot, under the surveillance and with the help of Mrs Galsworthy, shortly after her husband's death. After such a brief lapse of time the information it contained had necessarily to be kept within certain limits; within them, this is a detailed, accurate and voluminous record of Galsworthy's life. Among several books of personal reminiscence the two I found most valuable were *Memories of John Galsworthy* by his sister, M. E. Reynolds, published three years after he died; and *For Some We Loved*, by R. H. Mottram the novelist, a warm-hearted account of his life-long friendship with both Galsworthy and his wife. Mrs Galsworthy wrote, after her husband's death, two books of personal memories, *Over the Hills and Far Away* and *Our Dear Dogs*, which contain some interesting glimpses of their life together.

From these sources, personal and recorded, I have gathered the facts for my book; the opinions expressed in it are of course entirely my own.

BIBLIOGRAPHY

Our Dear Dogs by Ada Galsworthy (Scribner's, 1936; reprinted by St Catherine Press, 1953)

Over the Hills and Far Away by Ada Galsworthy (Robert Hale, 1937)

Letters from John Galsworthy, 1900 to 1932 by Edward Garnett (Jonathan Cape, 1934)

A Bibliography of the Works of John Galsworthy by H. V. Marrot (Franklin Book, 1928)

The Life and Letters of John Galsworthy by H. V. Marrot (Heinemann, 1935)

John Galsworthy by R. H. Mottram (London House, 1953)

For Some We Loved by R. H. Mottram (Fernhill, 1956)

John Galsworthy by Herman Ould (Chapman and Hall, 1934)

Memories of John Galsworthy by his sister, M. E. Reynolds (Robert Hale, 1936)

John Galsworthy, A Survey by Leon Schalt (Scribner's, 1929)

I

On many a morning in the last years of the reign of King Edward VII a man of middle age could be seen seated on the south-facing veranda of a small, somewhat dank Devon farmhouse on the edge of Dartmoor, writing vigorously on a pad of paper resting on his knee. He was of slight build and medium height, with thinning hair and well-shaped features set off by a monocle in his right eye, in which he was genuinely short-sighted. He was writing, as was his invariable custom, with a penholder containing a J nib which he periodically dipped into an inkpot by his side on the paving stones of the veranda. At his other side lay a black spaniel dog; his love for dogs was almost exaggeratedly English. In a stable in the farmyard at the rear of the building stood his horse, Peggy. Horse-riding was the exercise to which he was keenly devoted throughout his life.

As he wrote, there came through the window behind him the sound of a piano being played softly but exquisitely by his wife. Her skill as a pianist fell only just short of the standards of the concert platform. She was probably playing Mozart or perhaps an aria. He liked music with a tune to it. Whatever it was, he liked it played softly. Wagner he could not abide. If she paused, he would call, "Go on, go on, Ada. Don't stop." The music would begin again, the spaniel, having raised its head, would contentedly lower it and John Galsworthy would continue to write the novel of English manners upon which he was engaged.

The woman at the piano contributed far more, however, than a background of music to the composition of the long series of novels and plays which in his own lifetime placed Galsworthy at the head of contemporary English literature, and which includes one trilogy, *The Forsyte Saga*, as certain to endure as any novel in the English language. In the first place, it was she who persuaded him to attempt a writing career, although there was not at that time the slightest indication that he had any talent for it. He was simply a briefless barrister in his late twenties, living idly on an allowance from his father, a wealthy solicitor, and unhappy at the aimlessness of his life. She and he were then at the beginning of an agonizing, passionate, furtive love affair which was to continue for some ten years, during most of which time she went on living in the house of her first husband, Major Arthur Galsworthy, a cousin of her lover. During those years she—and, for a time, she alone—encouraged him to persevere at the task of writing fictional stories, for which he seemed quite unfitted. Most of the early stories he published are naïve, amateurish and derivative. But she kept him to the work and by the time the love affair had ended in a divorce which enabled John and Ada Galsworthy to marry, he had with her constant help mastered his art. During the months of waiting for the divorce to become absolute, he wrote the last third of a novel, *The Man of Property*, which can fairly be measured against acknowledged classics, and which added the Forsytes to the company of the enduring characters of English fiction.

Ada also gave him his basic themes. Before he fell in love with her, he had felt a vague, idle kind of wish to be able to write. In a letter to another young woman with whom he conducted philosophical discussions in a serious, youthful manner, he had remarked, "I do wish I had the gift of writing, I really think that is the nicest way of making money going, only it isn't really the writing so much as the thoughts that one wants; and, when you feel like a very shallow pond, with no nice cool deep pools with queer and pleasant things at the bottom, what's the good? I suppose one could cultivate writing, but one can't cultivate clear depths and quaint plants."

He wrote that about six months before he fell in love with his cousin's wife and about a year before they became lovers. The upheaval supplied the deficiency. Now he had something to write about—a protest against the cruelty that chained a sensitive woman to an unhappy marriage and indeed, against the whole hypocrisy of moneyed society in late Victorian and Edwardian England. As he struggled to construct one book after another while their affair remained secret, he touched, slightly and irrelevantly at first, upon this theme; then more strongly and boldly; and at last, with Ada's consent and help, had the courage to make it the central purpose of a novel and achieved *The Man of Property*. While he was writing it, he and Ada were suffering the ostracism and scandal which, with the stricter propriety of that time, attended a divorce. It is curious that Galsworthy's career as a man of letters, which was to lead to the Order of Merit and the Nobel Prize for Literature, was founded upon and sustained by a series of events in his young manhood which compelled him to resign from the Junior Carlton Club.

In all his work Ada was intimately bound. Whenever he was writing, she was near at hand. With her he discussed every thought, every sentence, translating into the terms of fiction the physical and mental experience they had known together. He never had a secretary; Ada took all his drafts and typed them to provide him with fair copies of each day's work for the interminable processes of revision to which, in consultation with her, he subjected every line. Short of actually holding the pen, she seems almost to have participated in the writing, a collaborator so close and intimate that her contribution was integral to the structure. As a curious illustration, at one time Galsworthy, possibly contemplating autobiography, assembled into two notebooks an outline account of several years of their life together. The handwriting is hers (she often wrote from his dictation). The per-

11

sonal pronouns are mixed. In one sentence the writer can change from "he" to "I", from "J.G." to "we", from "A.G." to "me"; as though the diaries were being kept by a composite being with four hands.

To her intimate participation in his life and his work he responded with an intense personal devotion. She was a fervent hypochondriac but he nursed every imagined ill with deep and tender care. Although he detested travelling, he spent each winter wandering dutifully through the warmer parts of the world, convinced that Ada's health would not sustain the rigours of the English climate; after his death she spent most of her remaining winters in England and she survived him by twenty-two years. As a wealthy man he could surround her with luxury and servants, but he also devoted his personal attention to furthering her every whim, sometimes to absurdity. A nephew remembers beating Ada one evening at a game of billiards, a favourite family game. Galsworthy led him gently away into a corner to tell him privately, "You must understand, my dear old man, that in this house Aunty always wins."

This solicitude for her, this devotion to the point of the ridiculous was, however, his strength as a writer, the essence of him. He was regarded as a powerful critic of the ruling class of his time, labelled in his day a revolutionary and once called the most dangerous man in England, but in all respects save one his was a palace revolution. He was generous and charitable with the wealth he inherited but he remained a wealthy man. He attacked the class into which he had been born but never thought of forgoing its privileges. His motives and inspiration were not social but personal. This he knew and once admitted in a letter to Edward Garnett. The novels were "simply the criticism of one half of myself by the other ... not a piece of social criticism". The one half of himself was all Forsyte—rich, privileged, and with a deep horror of any threatening change. The other was the young man of passion who fell inextricably in love with a married woman and suffered, for her as well as himself, the social consequences inevitable at that time. So long as Ada was despised and shunned by their world, so long was Galsworthy an angry, protesting rebel. Before the First World War he depicted Soames Forsyte as the man of property, exerting the rights of ownership upon his unwilling wife—a character for whom Galsworthy could feel pity but never forgiveness. Nevertheless, his instinctive purpose was not to upset Forsyte society but to bring Ada safely back into its warmth and comfort. After the war, an England which had looser moral standards accepted the writer who was becoming celebrated together with his wife and the scandal of twenty years earlier was forgotten.

There was no more rebel in Galsworthy then. When he began to extend *The Man of Property* into the chronicles of a family which became *The Forsyte Saga*, he did so with compassion and humanity, with gentle humour and more than a touch of nostalgia, but with no protest. Soames Forsyte grew through each succeeding book until he became the central figure of the chronicle and, as he grew, he became ever more certainly the mouthpiece of his author. All the opinions which the ageing Soames expresses in the later Forsyte novels are those which his family recall having heard John Galsworthy himself utter. The man of property, who in 1906 represented all that Ada had suffered, was not only forgiven by his author; he was gradually merged with him. By the time of the general strike of 1926, Soames Forsyte was no longer pitied or condemned or despised by John Galsworthy. By then Soames Forsyte was John Galsworthy and there could be little ahead for the novelist but honorary doctorates, honours and the highest public esteem for his services to Literature.

II

The most important person in John Galsworthy's childhood was his father, old John Galsworthy, the model for old Jolyon Forsyte.

His ancestors, on tracing whom his son spent thirty years of his life and considerable trouble and money, are known to have been, since the sixteenth century, small farmers living close by the sea in south Devon around Wembury and Plymstock. There is a farmhouse on a cliff where the family dwelt and a field still known as Great Galsworthy, pronounced with a short "a"; it was the novelist who changed the pronunciation to a long "a", having convinced himself that he had found some Old English derivation for it.

Not all the ancestors remained on the farm. Some came to London and found a more profitable use for land—they speculated and built upon it. The novelist's grandfather, also named John, had been a merchant at Plymstock but when his wife died he brought his children to London and engaged in the new family occupation of property investment. Old John, the novelist's father, was articled in his youth to a solicitor, and practised as such in the City of London throughout his life, though he despised his profession and would have preferred to have gone to the Bar. He enlivened and varied his lot, however, by accepting active directorships in several companies, some of them engaged in mining in Canada and in Russia. He was a respected but dominating and somewhat feared man in the City. He had the luck, as his son pointed out, to have lived in "that moneymaker's Golden Age, the nineteenth century". Even so, he did unusually well, accumulating a six-figure fortune, much of which he invested, with the family talent, in house and shop property. At his peak he was reputed to have an income of £12,000 a year, a sum of prodigious purchasing power at that time.

Three portraits have been left of him, all slightly sentimental and idealized, but combining to portray him in his old age —the period in which he was most loved—as a man of strength and gentleness, power and some wisdom and a deep love of children. The first and best known is the fictional portrait, that is old Jolyon in The Forsyte Saga, "the head of the family, eighty years of age, with his fine, white hair, his dome-like forehead, his little, dark gray eyes, and an immense white moustache, which drooped and spread below the level of his strong jaw". The immense white moustache was in fact a full white flowing beard and moustaches. Otherwise this picture of old Jolyon tallies exactly with both the others of old John.

One of these is another word sketch by his novelist son, "A Portrait", published in a collection of sketches, A Motley, in 1910, six years after his father's death. It was written in the full warmth of posthumous affection but there is more than a hint that old John's business conduct, while of course of the utmost integrity, did not lack vigour. He was splendidly dignified and courageous "when facing an awkward General Meeting". On the boards on which he served there was one other man of like calibre with whom conflicts were, it seems, frequent; old John always won the victory, though he was "the quicker tempered and more cautious". He was indeed a hasty-tempered man. He was also a lonely man, largely cut off from friendships, as his son was after him: "In his long life he made singularly few fast friendships with grown-up people, and, as far as I know, no enemies. For there was in him, despite his geniality, a very strong vein of fastidiousness, and such essential deep love of domination, that he found, perhaps, few men of his own age and standing to whom he did not feel natively superior."

As parallel, there is a description by a Harrow schoolmaster of John Galsworthy, the novelist, returning to his old school in his later years, as he frequently did, to watch the cricket: "He comes on to the field. He sits and watches the play. He doesn't speak to a soul; and when the match is over for the day, he gets up and walks away. Why don't I go up and talk to him? Oh, I don't like to thrust myself on a distinguished man like that."

In his family life, old John was distinguished by a devoted love of all children and particularly of his own: "With them he became completely tender, inexhaustibly interested in their interests, absurdly patient, and as careful as a mother. No child ever resisted him, or even dreamed of so doing. . . . [He had] perfect identification with whatever might be the matter in hand. The examination of a shell, the listening to the voice of the sea imprisoned in it, the making of a cocked hat out of *The Times* newspaper, the doing up of little buttons, the feeding of pigeons with crumbs, the holding fast of a tiny leg while walking beside a pony, all these things absorbed him completely, so that no visible trace was left of the man whose judgment on affairs was admirable and profound. Nor, whatever the provocation, could he ever bring himself to point the moral of anything to a child, having that utter toleration of their foibles which only comes from a natural and perfectly unconscious love of being with them."

The third portrait of old John, done in oils by Georg Sauter, a Bavarian painter of more than ordinary gifts who married one of his daughters, shows him with a child, Rudolf Sauter, his grandson. The child, still young enough to have his hair flowing to his shoulders, stands with his arm around the shoulder of the old man with huge white beard and gentle eyes. They are looking at a large sea-shell (a relic which the grandson possesses to this day).

Many years later, Galsworthy told the child that it was this portrait, with the beard subtracted, which he held in mind as his conception of the appearance of old Jolyon Forsyte.

There is one strange omission from all three portraits of old John: his wife. She is not in the painting. In the novel old Jolyon is alone. In the sketch there is the single sentence, "He did not marry till he was forty-five, but his feeling for the future of his family manifested itself with the birth of his first child." Of the wife nothing is said. Yet she was no pale nonentity.

With his passion for his family tree, Galsworthy devoted even more attention to his mother's ancestors than to his father's but with less success. Blanche Bailey Bartleet, as she was born, came from a line in which mingled country squires, needlemakers of Redditch and gentleman farmers in Cambridgeshire. The line could be traced back to an eighteenth-century needlemaker, and then remained obstinately obscure. Galsworthy could conjecture that the family was part of that of the Worcestershire Bartleets, or Bartlets, of Castle Morton, one of whom was physician to Henry VIII, and even, possibly, one of the Sussex Bartelots, who came over with William the Conqueror, but he could not prove it. There was, he conjectured, a bastardy in the line. He composed a few wry outlines of his maternal uncles: the one who would not go into business and was all for horses and went to Australia to be killed in a riding accident; the one who was a tea-planter in India ("there is nothing like the *best* Indian tea"); the one who, after training as a solicitor, "revolted into the Church", and "was addicted to microscopes, chess, homeopathy, intermittent teetotalism and vegetarianism, and the theory that Bacon wrote Shakespeare"; and so on. This was the side of his ancestry, Galsworthy once told Edward Garnett, from which he supposed he got his sense of form. It was from the Galsworthys that he felt he derived his creative energy.

Like a dutiful son, he left three portraits of his mother, one

17

factual and two fictional, all in terms of polite respect, with little sign of affection. At best, he regretted his inability to feel more warmly towards her; at worst, he found her irritating and silly. There are also two portraits of her by Georg Sauter which make much the same points. One is in profile, the other full face, and they were both done when she was in her late fifties; she was twenty years younger than her husband. Both show a woman tiny in stature, immaculate in appearance, stern and determined in expression, with lips pressed thinly together, eyes unsmiling, hair grey. The profile wears a somewhat mean expression. A sketch of her once led somebody to declare that she looked like a French *marquise* and the description stuck. In fact she had spent much of her girlhood in France, at first at school in Paris and later as a companion for a valetudinarian father, and she retained throughout her life a love for all things French, particularly if they were clothes.

Galsworthy, in the factual sketch he wrote four years after her death, did his best to seem a loving son: "She was a wonderfully good and careful manager of our big house, and a wonderful mother. But, looking back at that dim time, it seems to me that we saw but little of her, and I suspect that a husband, a house with eight indoor and six outdoor servants, much entertaining, a large garden (she was devoted to flowers), *et hoc omne* took too much of her time, and her health was not very good in those days." Almost his earliest memory of her was "of a scented and graciously dressed presence at good night kiss times". The children saw little more of her, except on the Sunday morning drive to church. Her son noted that "the Queen, the Royal family, the Church, the structure of Society, all to her were final". She read little, but rode well, and could hold her own at archery. She was "a charming figurehead for a dinner-table", and although she was not arrogant, "people of gentle blood were clearly to her different in species to those not of gentle blood." He wrote, "I loved my mother, and she loved me; and yet we were never very close. . . . We could not get on terms of mental approach. Between her and my father there was, I am sure, the same difficulty, and after a few years their married life was not really a happy one. She could not help trying to exact from those about her a conformity to her very precise and sometimes (as it would seem to us) narrow standards of taste. My father's will and hers were both exceptionally strong; neither could really yield to the other. Then I have always been exceptionally independent in mind, and given to spiritual claustrophobia. The result was an unbridgeable gap, almost on my part an avoidance, because I soft-heartedly hated not to respond and yet knew I could not. Almost at once—if we talked—a kind of irritation would begin in me, a sort of inward railing at the closed door I perceived in her mind. It was a grief that I had in my mother an exceptional woman of strong and high character, and a great flavour of her own, and yet not to be able to appreciate and exploit her —as it were—except aesthetically in a detached way. My father really predominated in me from the start, and ruled my life. I was so truly and deeply fond of him that I seemed not to have a fair share of love left to give my mother. One cannot see oneself, but I have often wondered what I got from her—not her stoic endurance, nor firmness of will, piety (if that be a virtue), her patience, her self-denying care for others. Verily I believe all I got from her was a capacity and almost a liking for nursing, and perhaps my critical sense; the rest of me is, I think, my father's. Looking back on her, I see how notable and admirable she was," he gallantly adds; "one always, indeed, admired her. Just that lack of speculation in her divided us. What a pity for me!"

This was a charitable portrait, done by a man with the kindest of natures. When he came to fictional portrayals, he could not avoid bringing out the essential pettiness of the woman.

She was avowedly the model for Frances Freeland in the fifth and last of his critical novels of late Victorian and Edwardian society, *The Freelands*. He wrote it when, in her seventy-seventh year, she was living at an hotel in Torquay in failing health and he knew she was near her end. In his diary he commented, "Her illness was wonderfully borne; she never once said a word about going, or made moan." But his true epitaph for his mother was Frances Freeland, a portrait that, in such circumstances, was naturally sentimentalized: "A sudden vision came to him of his mother's carved ivory face, kept free of wrinkles by sheer will-power, its firm chin, slightly aquiline nose, and measured brows; its eyes which saw everything so quickly, so fastidiously; its compressed mouth which smiled sweetly, with a resolute but pathetic acceptation. Of the piece of fine lace, sometimes black, sometimes white, over her grey hair. Of her hands, so thin now, always moving a little, as if all the composure and care, not to offend any eye by allowing Time to ravage her face, were avenging themselves in that constant movement. Of her figure, certainly short but not seeming so, still quick-moving, still alert, and always dressed in black or grey. A vision of that exact, fastidious, wandering spirit ... strangely compounded of domination and humility, of acceptation and cynicism; precise and actual to the point of desert dryness; generous to a degree which caused her family to despair; and always, beyond all things, brave."

At another point in the novel, Frances Freeland has just made a long journey, and, nobody having realized that she has eaten nothing all day, she tells nobody, though "for want of a cup of tea her soul was nearly dying within her". She sits very still, "knowing by long experience that to indulge oneself in private only made it more difficult not to indulge oneself in public. . . . She took from her pocket a tiny prayer-book, and, holding it to the light, read the eighteenth psalm —it was a particularly good one, which never failed when she felt low—she used no glasses, and up to the present had avoided any line between the brows, knowing it was her duty to remain as nice as she could to look at, so as not to spoil the pleasure of people round about her. Saying firmly to herself, 'I do not, I *will* not want any tea—but I shall be glad of dinner!' she rose and opened her cane trunk." Then she "sat down again to be quite quiet for a moment, with her still-dark eyelashes resting on her ivory cheeks and her lips pressed to a colourless line; for her head swam from stooping over. In repose, with three flies circling above her fine grey hair, she might have served a sculptor for a study of the stoic spirit."

But Galsworthy could not keep out of the novel his customary irritation with his mother. Frances Freeland is little more than a nuisance to the Freeland family, always giving everybody silly little presents which nobody wants, never having the least understanding of the emotional crises through which they are passing and taking charge of a sickroom with that kind of efficient, motherly self-sacrifice that compels the patient to bite his lips to prevent a shriek of exasperation.

In the other fictional portrait of her, the short story, "The Grey Angel", which he wrote after her death, Galsworthy was just as sentimental but even less able to keep out a sense of her silliness. The grey angel is an elderly lady living in France during the First World War, who devotes herself to taking small gifts to the wounded in a nearby French military hospital. This becomes such an obsession that, denying herself even sufficient food in order to be able to continue her generosity, she at last forces herself into a double pneumonia of which she dies. It is, of course, the wounded men who nickname her *"L'ange aux cheveux gris"*, although the gifts she takes them are mostly useless to them—"some English riddles translated by herself into French (very curious), some ancient copies of an illustrated paper, boxes of chocolate, a ball of string to make 'cats' cradles' (such an amusing game), her own packs of patience cards, some photograph frames, postcards of Arles, and, most singular, a kettle holder." And the grey hair, by the way, is a wig. This whole portrait of Blanche Galsworthy is full of mockery: "Unto her seventy-eighth year, her French accent had remained unruffled, her soul in love with French gloves and dresses; and her face had the pale, unwrinkled, slightly aquiline perfection of the French *marquise* type—it may, perhaps, be doubted whether any French *marquise* ever looked the part so perfectly." She did not exactly worry about the war, "she only grieved quietly over the dreadful things that were being done, and every now and then would glow with admiration at the beautiful way the King and Queen were behaving". In her illness, she refuses to be kept from going to church (" 'How do you suppose our dear little Queen in England would get on with all she has to do, if she were to give in like that?' ") although, once there, the effort seems pointless. "She was not clever, and never even began to try and understand what she believed. If she tried to be good she would go to God—wherever God might be—and rarely did she forget to try to be good. Sitting there, she thought or rather prayed: 'Let me forget that I have a body, and remember the poor soldiers'."

It was not only on her son John that Mrs Galsworthy had this irritating effect. With the exception of two of her grandchildren to whom she was especially devoted and who were equally devoted to her, her fussiness, primness and narrowness of mind drove most of her family to distraction. She took very little notice of her children when they were young. Galsworthy was always, as a boy, intensely bored with the holidays he had to spend at home and anxious to return to school, where life was interesting. His sisters found her meticulousness almost unendurable. She was continually adjusting the set of the girls' dresses, or correcting some slightly slipshod expression they had uttered. She liked everything to be formal rather than natural. For instance, she always did her best to prevent the children from getting sun-tanned on a seaside holiday; she liked their skins to be pale, not brown. It was once said of her that "her diamonds were always correct".

As her children grew up, they found her more and more wearing. One of her daughters, Lilian, despaired so much at the thoughts of exasperation and worse that her mother roused in her that on June 5, 1887, when she was in her early twenties, she confided to her diary, "I wonder if it would lessen the acuteness of nervous irritation and aching which one incompatibility causes, to myself (and I imagine also to Mother), if I try and analyse it and, at any rate, put my feelings down!

"I wonder if it is purely physical, the process that takes place in me at times, set in action by her presence. I lie on the sofa thinking or reading, she comes in, says a word or two or perhaps not even that, cuts a pencil, walks about the room tidying up, looks at her plants, or even sits in her arm chair reading and simply swings her foot; nothing more, even less, even her very presence, if the excitement has already been set up, is enough to produce this effect: a feeling of complete inability to fix my thoughts on the subject of study, a horrible apprehension that the next moment will bring a remark, and that remark a small external criticism, sets up excitement of all my nerves, I shut my eyes but I still see her, I try to exclude the subtle influence, which usually has no effect but the apparent tightening of my nerves resulting in positive pain and soreness all over.

"I do not think I ever have experienced this in the same

degree from contact with any one else, but that is probably through my never having been thrown so much with another.

"The fault, if fault there be, is as much, I am convinced, on one side as the other, but I am inclined to think that it is a matter beyond our control.... Physically I should think we are similarly constituted, neither strong, both nervous, whether the different construction of our brains would account for it I don't know, but I *think* it must be the different construction of our egos. Our characters (each as a whole) afford a striking contrast and it is interesting to me to study the parallel, with the points of con and divergence the comparison is the clue to many assortments of character I come across, with their riddles of compatibility and antagonism.

"The principal difference, the 'great gulf' fixed between us, is this:

"1. My mind is essentially introspective, contemplative. (I am all through using 'mind' for entire ego):

"2. Mother's mind is essentially the reverse. Her organs of sight and sound and touch and the corresponding mental faculties are extraordinarily quick; and her critical faculty strongly developed, though developed almost entirely with use upon outward objects.

"It is a perfectly consistent mind and this key: *externality* (not triviality) unlocks the whole. I say it is not a trivial mind, for it is serious with religious and emotional if not intellectual depths; but yet in one sense, it is so, for it is more commonly and completely occupied with trifles, more acutely sensible of petty matters than is compatible with any greatness....

"By externality I mean acute observation of and concentration of the mind upon outward things, not an absence of reflection. The external mind exercises itself most congenially with household matters, it *excels* in domestic duties of

24

housekeeping and dressmaking; the arrangement of rooms, dresses and dinners and the management of servants etc. take a surprising amount of mind but of the external kind. . . .

"The external mind in its religious phase is full of feeling, warm impulse and promptings to duty, but all attach themselves to outward objects: the outward forms of religion are *much* to such a mind, the outward demonstrations of affection much, duties are clearly defined, strongly binding, not only upon itself but in its opinion upon others; its creed, too, after it has taken perhaps some little pains to get '*the right*' one, is binding, becomes more or less a dogma.

"The external mind is infinitely pained by untidiness and attaches the greatest importance I have noticed to the following details; threads and pins being left about, books, papers, etc., not put away, mistakes in grammar, spelling or etiquette, above all small points crooked, or wrong in personal appearance

"Whenever you go near this mind you feel as if you were nearing a large microscope and life becomes immediately a burden to the unhappy being whose hair is not becomingly 'done', who has a pin or a stitch showing, or not, or, most hopeless of all, whose dress whobbles! So entirely exclusively and quickly does this mind seize these details that if you come to it with a face full of trouble (or a heart presumably to match below) or a manner full of interest, (with a question one might imagine of equal interest behind) you will be greeted (and perhaps chilled and placed a little further from the range of future sympathy, who knows), by the remark, 'don't walk with your legs tied together; you turn your toes in and twist your legs about in the funniest way'! or . . . 'You haven't pinned your dress straight, how many more times shall I have to tell you'. . . .

"I go up to some one of this nature with an important

question or remark; it is like facing a fusilade; the glaze of the external eye is on my bonnet! and a myriad little thoughts are busy within upon the rearrangement of feathers or bow. What a tremendous freak it's in—would that I would take it off and let it be altered just a little!

"O, never mind, if I like to go a perfect fright, and, as I whisk out of the door in a hurry, 'come back one minute and let me put a pin in your dress, it's all on one side, and look here at this great piece of ravelling—I never saw such an untidy child, why can't you look in the glass and keep yourself nice!'

"And I—am the very reverse of all this, no practical good at all—as unobservant as an old bat and as lazy as any one can well be—a dreamer who occasionally thinks, and acts seldom and with extreme difficulty. A kind of mind who can walk straight into a drawing-room at a dinner party with goloshes on."

One other characteristic of their mother which neither Galsworthy nor his sister cared to mention was her jealousy of her husband. It seems to have become in the end an obsession. Towards the close of their married life she accused him of taking too great an interest in the young governess of one of his grandsons. Although, at the time, old John was eighty-six years of age, his wife left him. She moved from his house into a flat at Kensington Palace Mansions. He went to the house of a married daughter and there he died, without Blanche ever coming back to live with him.

This, then, was the end of the marriage that had started nearly forty years earlier, when he was in his forty-fifth year, and she in her twenty-fifth. The home in which Galsworthy grew up, and which had such an obvious influence on his writing as well as upon his private life, was that of a dearly loved father and a disliked mother, who were unhappy between themselves. It is not difficult to detect the first cause of the sense of guilt which deeply coloured at least the first half of his adult life, and which, aggravated by the social defiance of his own love affair, drove him to the five novels of protest, and in particular to *The Man of Property* and the creation of the Forsytes.

III

It would be quite wrong, however, to depict Galsworthy's youthful home as an unhappy one. While the children were young, the stresses were buried in the love with which old John fed his children and in the wealth with which he provided them.

When old John married Blanche Bartleet in 1862, he took her to live in London, first at Mansfield Street and then to a house, since knocked down, in Portland Place. But when within a couple of years their first child, Lilian, was born, he decided at once to move out into country air and surroundings. Kingston Hill in Surrey which was then surrounded by open countryside with a few large houses placed here and there was his choice. First he took a double-fronted, porticoed mansion called Parkfield, to serve as a base while he looked for a site on which to build. At Parkfield his second child, John, was born on August 14, 1867.

Old John had by then bought his building site at Coombe Warren, close by. He took a long lease on twenty-four acres, high on the hill, looking across to the North Downs at a distance of about fifteen miles; sometimes the grandstand at Epsom race-course could just be seen. On this site he built, at intervals of some years, three large solid Victorian houses. The first, which he named Coombe Warren—an ornate house of brick, mullion windows, gables and a kind of spire pierced by a dormer window, standing on a terrace at the head of the slope—was ready for the family soon after young John's birth. There the two other children, Hubert and Mabel, were born. As they grew up, their father built the two other houses adjoining Coombe Warren—named, in turn, Coombe Leigh and Coombe Croft—and they lived in one or other of them until 1886, by which time John, the elder son, was nineteen years of age. They then returned to London.

While they lived on Kingston Hill, old John devoted as much of his time as possible to his children. His solicitor's firm in Old Jewry and the companies he directed seem to have demanded of him only an easy working week. He went to town every morning at eleven and returned at five in the afternoon and he kept Saturdays as well as Sundays free for Coombe. The station that he used was Coombe and Malden, reached in a T-cart driven by Haddon, the family's coachman.

Old John's presence permeated Coombe. One of his daughters, Mabel, many years later recalled him, with a small child's hand in his, making his rounds of the gardens, paddocks and little home-farmyard, stroking the cows, watching the chickens and baby pigs, peering into bushes for the latest birds' nests. His son John recorded that the place was an endless pleasure to him and recalled how "quite wonderful was the forethought he lavished on that house and little estate stretching down the side of the hill, with its walled gardens, pasture, cornland and coppice. All was solid, and of the best, from the low four-square red brick house with its concrete terrace and French windows, to the cow-houses down by the coppice. From the oak trees, hundreds of years old, on the lawns, to the peach trees just planted along the south sunny walls.... Everything was at hand, from home-baked bread, to mushrooms wild and tame; from the stables with their squat clock-tower, to pigsties; from roses that won all the local prizes, to bluebells; but nothing redundant or pretentious." In his description of this Victorian paradise where he spent his childhood, Galsworthy makes no mention of his mother. But his sister Mabel gives one glimpse of her, "constantly on the sofa with a piece of black Spanish lace over her head. Gentle and loving, devoted to her husband and children

... our mother nevertheless is not so prominent and everyday a figure as our father in the hazy memory of those early days."

Galsworthy used Coombe, of course, as the model for Robin Hill, the country setting for the Forsytes. The grounds and coppice of Coombe Warren were the site of the Forsyte house, but its architecture was imaginary.

Young John and his brother went to a preparatory school named Saugeen at Bournemouth and, during the summer holidays, played cricket on Coombe lawn. When he was thirteen years of age, John went to Harrow. He proved a good footballer and athlete, but no more than a fair scholar; there was the letter to his parents, of the kind traditionally expected from the housemaster of any boy who is to become a famous man of letters, that "if only he was not so weak in composition he might really distinguish himself at Harrow". He duly became head of his house, and Captain of the School at football. Many years later he himself declared that he had passed at Harrow "on the whole a happy time" but "we were debarred from any real interest in philosophy, history, art, literature and music, or any advancing notions in social life or politics; we were reactionaries almost to a boy." He summed the thing up in a reference in *The Freelands* to "the mills of gentility— those unique grinding machines of education only found in his native land".

The only slightly surprising thing about Galsworthy's somewhat indifferent career at Harrow is that, when he left, his housemaster wrote him a letter in effusive terms of admiration: "I can honestly say to you that I never expect to be able to replace your loss; and I have never had amongst many good heads one who was at once more easy to work with than yourself, and so completely to my heart in every respect. I shall always look back to you, therefore, as my ideal head, without exaggeration." His headmaster, Dr Welldon, took a more moderate view. He recalled him as "a quiet, modest, unassuming boy ... a strictly honourable boy who made his mark both in work and play, without affording any notable promise of his distinction in after-life".

In his last years at school he had been, as an old friend remarked, "something of a swell". His outward appearance expressed the mould in which his mind had been formed— pressed by no particular ambition, indulging in very little independence of thought, and imbued with the conventionally honourable principles of the English public-schoolboy. He was simply an upright, arrogant young man of the wealthy upper-middle class, confident of his inheritance and his superiority, perfectly content to enjoy his privilege as of right and abiding strictly by the code of behaviour of his time and place.

In this temper he went up to New College, Oxford, in 1886, to embark upon a university career that was even less distinguished than his years at school. He read Law because his father had decided that he should be a barrister; he did not himself particularly care what he read, since he had no intention of serious study, and one school would serve as well as another as background to his social enjoyment. His only intensive reading was in the novels of Whyte Melville, from which he took his notions of university life. From being the best-dressed boy at Harrow he developed at Oxford into a dandy. His collars grew higher, his cravats more modish, the cut of his jacket more important to him. He confined himself to a small circle of friends of good class and superior form. He contributed nothing to the intellectual life of his college and, more surprisingly, nothing to its athletic activities. He had persuaded himself and his intimates that he had strained his heart from his running of races at school; medical nonsense, of course, but all part of his mental attitude. His exercise seems to have consisted largely of a foppish stroll along the

High Street, parading his elegant clothes. At this time, too, the short-sightedness of his right eye induced him to adopt a monocle, which he wore in public for the rest of his life (though in private he would drop it in favour of spectacles). His chief interest seems to have been horse-racing, and he was reputed to be one of the most knowledgeable men of his year on the subject of horses and racing form. In the course of this study, he naturally also acquired some debts to his bookmaker. He became a member of Vincent's and the Grid-iron, joined the O.U.D.S. but played only walking-on parts, rode as much as he could, occasionally to hounds, and generally led the life of a spark, a blood. He overspent his allowance of £300 from his father and regularly pawned his watch towards the end of every term. H. A. L. Fisher, the Warden of New College, who had been an undergraduate there at the same time as Galsworthy, was asked many years later to recall what he could of his fellow student, and found he could recall practically nothing except that he "led the conventional life of the well-to-do, not very intellectual undergraduate from a great Public School"; that he had a nonchalant and languid manner and was always the best-dressed man in College; that his knowledge of horse-racing was extensive; and that he "contented himself" with Second Class Honours in Jurisprudence.

When he went home for the vacations, he now went to London, for the family had moved at first into a flat in Kensington Palace Mansions and then into a house which old John built alongside Regent's Park. In partnership with one of his brothers and a builder, he built ten large houses in a row, and named them Cambridge Gate. Each partner kept three houses for himself and they shared the proceeds of the tenth. Old John let Nos 7 and 9 and set up his own household in No. 8, where he lived in style and fashion. Here Galsworthy found the background for the London life of the Forsytes, for although their houses are placed around Hyde Park, it is upon Cambridge Gate that they are modelled.

In the summer, the family rented houses in Switzerland for the mountains, or Scotland for the shooting, a sport at which young John excelled and which he intensely enjoyed. When he was not staying with his own parents, then he was a guest at the country houses of the families of his Oxford friends, indulging the same leisured tastes and acquiring a love for country-house theatricals. When he came down from Oxford in 1889, the kind of life he had led during the vacations simply spread itself throughout the year, except that he was reading for the Bar, to which he was called in the Easter term of 1890.

Throughout his Oxford period and for a couple of years afterwards, Galsworthy had been in love with a girl named Sybil Carr, whom he first met on a country-house visit in Wales. That is about all that is now known about her, except that she gave singing lessons, she was poor, and old John disapproved of her as a possible wife for his elder son. He was therefore sent off by his father to Canada, supposedly to inspect the coal mines of a company of which old John was chairman, but actually to get him out of the way of the singing teacher.

The Canadian tour, during which he joined his brother Hubert, who was also inspecting mines on Vancouver Island, was simply a holiday jaunt. It included a camping trip into the mountains under the care of an Indian guide, during which Galsworthy succeeded in getting himself lost in the forest and nearly drowned in one of the lakes. When he got back, he was still in love with Sybil, though the affair seems to have been more sustained than passionate. This was perhaps because, in the months that followed, he began at last to question the sort of life he had been educated to lead and which hitherto he had accepted as his due. He began to perceive the limits to his smug world of well-to-do gentility, in which sons were expected to do little but enjoy themselves on the incomes allowed them by their fathers, and daughters had to be kept so far as possible from any contamination by ideas.

The first disturbing factor was that his own sisters by no means conformed to this convention about daughters. Both Lilian and Mabel were girls of clear minds and vigorous wills. Neither had any intention of being restricted to domestic routines, as their mother would certainly have preferred; and fortunately they had, in their father, a loving champion of their desire to live more fully. One of the reasons for the removal of the family from Kingston Hill back to London was to enable Lilian to attend all the lectures, art galleries and concerts for which she craved. Lilian, fragile and slight in build, studious, sensitive in temperament, most seriously absorbed in writing and questions of philosophy and art, and ever attempting to write poetry, was the intellectual sister. Mabel, more robust and of a determined nature but perhaps just as sensitive, was intensely musical.

Into the lives of these two girls came Georg Sauter, the young Bavarian painter. A self-portrait of a slightly earlier date shows him as a wildly romantic young man, darkly handsome, Byronic. His story was as romantic as his appearance. Born into a peasant family in a small village in Bavaria, he was apprenticed as a boy to a man who decorated churches. An art patron who may have had some distant connection with his family was impressed by the young man's talent and sent him to the Academy at Munich, where he soon quarrelled with everybody, since his ideas of painting were at that time revolutionary. His patron therefore dispatched him to London to make a copy of the "Bacchus and Ariadne". An artistic young man engaged on such a task in the National Gallery inevitably met Lilian Galsworthy, who brought him home to Cambridge Gate—a stranger from a wildly different

34

world, almost inconceivable to the late-Victorian family into which he was introduced. Old John and Mrs Galsworthy were startled and probably apprehensive but, in deference to his daughters, old John grudgingly commissioned the young man to paint some portraits. He began on Mabel. It soon became apparent that she had fallen in love with him and for a time the family thought—and the parents feared—that they would make a match. But things turned out even worse. Georg Sauter was found not to be in love with Mabel but with Lilian and she with him. Mabel's distress can be imagined, her disappointment of a lover conflicting with her emotional loyalty to a beloved and devoted sister. But little, it seems, was said of the matter even at that time. No record of it other than a family memory has remained.

While all this was happening to the girls, Georg Sauter was also having a marked effect upon young John. It was the first time that he had come into intimate, domestic contact with the Artist, and he found it both exciting and disturbing. Here was a young man from nowhere, leading a life of absorbing purpose. How different from Galsworthy's own existence, the aimlessness of which was beginning to trouble him! How obviously satisfying! He contemplated with quite as much fascination as his sisters this young painter who, in the setting of Cambridge Gate, was not only strange in having an overwhelming purpose, but in that it had nothing to do with making money.

But this was not the only enlarging influence then at work upon young Galsworthy. There was the remarkable family of the Sandersons. Lancelot Sanderson, the father, was headmaster of a large preparatory school at Elstree. He was a man of frail health who kept as much as possible out of the way of his family of children; not surprisingly, since his ebullient Irish wife, Kitty, had presented him with sixteen, of whom thirteen survived into boisterous adolescence. Most of the thirteen were girls of strikingly handsome appearance, and the large house at Elstree was always full of young men who had come to admire them and would probably stay for a night or two and join in the vigorous, jolly life of the household. They habitually sat down in their private dining-room, Mabel Galsworthy noted, some twelve to fifteen persons to a meal, with a nurseryful of youngsters upstairs. Galsworthy was introduced into this energetic company—as energetic mentally as physically—by the eldest son, Ted, whom he had known at Harrow, and with whom he now developed a close friendship. Ted Sanderson's lively intellect was by no means unusual in this remarkable family or in the young men and women who gathered round them as visitors to the house. This invigorating atmosphere worked strongly upon Galsworthy, who went to the Sandersons' more and more frequently and began to hammer out religious, philosophical and artistic problems with Monica, the eldest daughter, who was probably the most striking of them all. Even now there are elderly men in London who can remember the vivid loveliness and the intellectual vigour of Monica Sanderson. One of them recalled her in a phrase that perhaps exactly expresses that formidably splendid person—"She used to sing in her cold bath." With this magnificent creature Galsworthy attained the warmest of intellectual friendships but never anything more. In 1892, indeed, he still thought himself in love with the young singing teacher, Sybil Carr, of whom old John still as strongly disapproved. His scheme of sending the young man on a trip to Canada to forget about her had not succeeded, but he had not lost confidence in the idea. Probably the separation had not been long enough. He therefore now suggested that, instead of continuing to read for the Chancery Bar, his son should turn to a study of navigation and maritime law and aim himself at the Admiralty Bar. It was a matter of complete indifference to Galsworthy as to which Bar he read for, since he had little interest in practising at any. But what his father proposed was a long sea voyage during which his maritime studies could best be carried on. The family was staying at a rented house in Scotland that summer when the suggestion was made, and Ted Sanderson, who was there as a guest, agreed to accompany his friend on a tour of Australia, New Zealand and the South Seas. What particularly persuaded Ted was the intention of visiting Samoa and the chance of meeting R. L. Stevenson; in fact they never did. The two young men therefore sailed in November in the Orient liner *Oruba* for Australia. Lilian and Mabel, ever of sympathetic natures, set themselves to console Sybil by getting her as many new singing pupils as they could and even by taking singing lessons themselves. As their brother noted in a letter he wrote to Lilian from New Zealand, "Thanks awfully, my dear old girl, for being so good about Mrs Carr and Sybil, it is a great relief to my mind to hear that pupils are coming in and that you have been able to do something. Awfully good of you to have lessons yourself, and very good of the governor to let you have them." Had this expression of gratitude been passed on to old John, no doubt he would have smiled quietly, for the longer journey had achieved his object. His son confided to Lilian, "Nothing will ever come of this matter between me and Sybil, I am too vague, and she doesn't care; all the better, really, you know, because I am not cut out for domesticity at first hand. However, go on and prosper in the matter of pupils and friendship."

He wrote this in a letter congratulating Lilian on her own engagement to Georg Sauter, news of which was to reach him when he had arrived at Auckland in February of the following year. The letter gives an idea of the stiltedness of his emotions at that time: "My dearest old girl, I am so glad to get your letter containing the good news, it is ripping for you, my dear, be blessed with my best love and good wishes. What a tremendous weight off your mind dear old girl. Please give Herr Sauter my best wishes and congratulations and shake him by the hand for me, and give him my heartiest welcome into the family. I must say I was a bit knocked out of true by the suddenness of the news, I knew it was going on right from May, but I didn't imagine you were going to have the luck to bring on a triumphant crisis so soon. I am awfully glad he's getting on so well and hope he will be an R.A. at least by the time I get back."

Even this was probably a warmer reception of the news than Lilian got from her parents. They were not in the least pleased that their elder daughter was to marry a young artist of dubious prospects. They did not approve of the match although they were aware that, with Lilian's determination on whatever she considered the right course, it would be futile actively to oppose it. What Mabel, the rejected sister, felt, nobody knows; but the incident contributed to the material which she offered to her brother when he was to use her as the model for the character of June Forsyte. All that can be said is that, with her inherent loyalty, she remained as firmly affectionate as ever to her sister Lilian.

IV

The journey of the two young men to the East was conducted in adventurous manner. After a halt in Ceylon, they sighted Australia in December 1892. From Sydney they took a dirty old tramp steamer for the Fiji Islands. On Suva they decided to sail by native cutter to the Ba river, where a remote cousin of the Galsworthys was planting sugar, and to trek back across the wild interior of one of the islands with a train of native porters. On the way, Ted Sanderson went down with dysentery. Galsworthy had to find him shelter in a village hut and nurse him as best he could until a runner could reach the coast with a message to send back drugs and instructions. At last Ted was carried out in a grass hammock on a long bamboo pole. Without the infinite care that Galsworthy took of him, he would, he said, probably have died on the way. However, he was got into a ship for New Zealand where he re-covered. On the way home the two young men sailed from Adelaide to Cape Town in the clipper *Torrens*, one of the most famous sailing ships of her time. By a coincidence that would disgrace any work of fiction, the first mate was Joseph Conrad, who had not yet had the courage to approach a publisher, but who already had the manuscript of *Almayer's Folly* locked in his cabin and had ventured to show it, un-finished, to one passenger, a Cambridge graduate named Jacques, who had encouraged him to complete it.

The meeting between Galsworthy, who had never so far given a thought to writing, and Conrad, who had not yet satisfied himself that he should try to publish, was to have very important consequences for them both, but at the time they made no unusual impression upon each other. Galsworthy's sister Mabel, writing long afterwards, declared there was no doubt that it was contact with Conrad's acutely observant, introspective type of brain and vivid speech which gave her brother's own mind its first push towards the appreciation of literature; but there is no evidence for it. Sanderson noted that they both used to keep the long watches with Conrad, when "there was any amount of opportunity for talk, Jack availed himself of this to the utmost.... Jack had missed Stevenson, but had found Conrad." But the suggestion that Galsworthy had recognized in Conrad a man of literary quality seems quite unfounded. The only mention of Conrad in two very long letters which he wrote home from the *Torrens*, is merely, "The first mate is a Pole called Conrad and is a capital chap, though queer to look at; he is a man of travel and experience in many parts of the world, and has a fund of yarns on which I draw freely. He has been right up the Congo and all around Malacca and Borneo and other out of the way parts, to say nothing of a little smuggling in the days of his youth." It seems certain, also, that Conrad saw nothing in Galsworthy that would persuade him to show the *Almayer* manuscript. The long friendship between Conrad and Ted Sanderson was founded during the voyage in the *Torrens*, but it was not until they all got home to England and Galsworthy found Conrad a frequent visitor to Elstree School—and *Almayer* shown now to everybody for discussion and emendation—that an enduring friendship was begun between those two.

During the voyage Galsworthy dutifully received daily instruction from the captain, immediately after breakfast, in taking sights of the sun; and for an hour each afternoon they discussed "manoeuvring and other seamanship questions". Whether the study of maritime law made as much progress is more doubtful; his reading was chiefly *The Count of Monte Cristo*—"six vols., in French"—and *The Story of an African*

Farm, which fascinated him. On his return to London, his further study of law was postponed by a journey to Russia upon which his father sent him. The trip was ostensibly to inspect some mines and to visit another Galsworthy cousin who, married to a Russian wife, was living in South Russia. This enabled the traveller to make his homeward journey through the Crimea, across the Black Sea to Constantinople and thus back to London, to settle uneasily to a further study of Admiralty Law. He read successively in two chambers in Lincoln's Inn. His own, when he set up in them in 1894, were in Paper Buildings in the Temple. Of his legal career there is almost nothing to relate. His father's firm of solicitors gave him a little work by joining him with a Q.C. when they wanted an "opinion". So far as is now known, he had only one brief, also from the firm of J. and E. H. Galsworthy, as junior to a Q.C. in an unopposed petition. When the case came on, he was strolling down the corridor, chatting to his father. The leading counsel made the petition, the judge granted it on the affidavits within a few minutes. The case ended before young Galsworthy knew it had begun, and his single opportunity to appear in court before a judge slipped from his grasp.

Rather earlier than this, he had left the family home and set himself up in a flat in Victoria Street, which he shared with a friend from Oxford, George Harris, who later entered Parliament. Old John had increased his allowance to £350 a year—this is the income he gave to each of his sons—and, in addition, young John may have received some small fees for attending board meetings of some of his father's companies, to which the latter was gradually introducing him.

In neither business nor the law, however, was the young man much interested. The influence of the Sanderson family and of their meetings and discussions, enriched now by the frequent presence of Conrad, lay strongly upon him. He spent as much time as he could at Elstree. He conducted long discussions with the splendid Monica, continuing them by letter when he was away in France or taking a holiday in Scotland accompanied by his first black spaniel, Lass; in London he had kept, rather guiltily, in his top-floor flat, a Skye terrier named Sylvia. The discussions were chiefly about religion, and Galsworthy was starting to take up an uneasily agnostic attitude, maintaining that, lacking faith, he found more virtue in courage: "Unless one conscientiously believes, it is childish to try to make oneself do so. The great thing, I take it, is to cultivate a stiff upper lip, both for the world's buffetings, and for what, if anything, we are going into, afterwards." Alongside these youthful arguments he displayed also, in his letters to Monica, the distaste which was creeping into him for the life he was leading and the kind of existence for which he seemed to be destined. "It does seem to me so beastly dull to go on grinding at a profession or business just to make money"; and he contemplated having a shy, with two or three other fellows, at the goldfields of Western Australia, where, with luck, one might in two or three years make enough for a lifetime: "I must say I should like to make some tin; it is an awful bore always being hard up more or less." This is the letter in which he makes his first mention of a wish to be able to earn his living as a writer, a possibility which he at once dismissed as out of his powers.

But in addition to that of the Sandersons there were two other influences which were moulding his mind and would soon start to shape his whole life.

The first was the discovery of intense poverty which existed all around him in London, alongside the small world of substantial wealth in which he himself moved. Old John set his elder son, on occasion, to the task of collecting rents. There no longer exists a complete record of the house property which the old man owned but some of it, probably in Fulham and

North Kensington, must have been slum housing. Galsworthy repeatedly told his wife, many years later, how distressed he had been to discover the living conditions of some of the people from whom the family's wealth was partly derived. The slums of London became an obsession with him. Harris, with whom he shared the flat in Victoria Street, has related how, night after night, he set off alone to wander through "the poorer districts, listening to the conversations of the people, sometimes visiting doss-houses". The degradation that he saw and the theme of inequality were to run all through most of the novels which he struggled to write during the next ten years. Harris declared that Galsworthy did not evince any particular interest in social questions or in politics (and rather aggrievedly recalls that when he was himself a candidate in the Election of 1895, and returned to their flat on Election night, he found Galsworthy reading a book and not even troubling to inquire the result of the poll). But these searchings into the slums at night had in fact thrust upon him a struggle of conscience in which an essentially political man —though never a party man—was formed. One of the novels, *The Island Pharisees,* is indeed a portrait of himself in his mid-twenties and of this struggle to discover principles which would enable him to tolerate his own sheltered privilege. It is the story of a well-to-do young man, Richard Shelton, who has been called to the Bar after coming down from Oxford, has "chucked" it (as Galsworthy himself was to do), is now seeking some accommodation with life and can find nothing but dust. "We are mean, that's what the matter with us," he cries, "dukes and dustmen, the whole human species—as mean as caterpillars. To secure our own property and our comfort, to dole out our sympathy according to rule, just so that it won't really hurt us, is what we're all after. There's something about human nature that is awfully repulsive, and the healthier people are, the more repulsive they seem to be."

He gazes upon his old school and college friends in his club: "What had there been to teach them anything of life? Their imbecility was incredible when you came to think of it. They had all the air of knowing everything and really they knew nothing—nothing of Nature, Art or the Emotions; nothing of the bonds that bind all men together.... They had a fixed point of view over life because they came from certain Schools and Colleges and Regiments! And they were those in charge of the State, of Laws, of Science, of the Army, and Religion." He goes to the fashionable wedding of one of his fellows and is conscious, as the bride enters the church, of "a shiver running through the audience which reminded him of a bullfight he had seen in Spain". This world of the upper middle class which has imbibed a taste for smart society has resulted in "a kind of heavy froth, an air of thoroughly domestic vice". Shelton himself is in love with a girl of this class for whom he feels a continual sexual desire, but whose response to the only kiss he ever ventures is a frigid terror.

How is he to tolerate his life? That is the unspoken question that gnaws at Shelton throughout the book. The best advice any of his friends can give him is, "You ought to *do* something, you know; it'll be fatal for you to have nothing to do.... I tell you what, you ought to stand for the County Council."

The tormented young man tries to break out of his own world by plunging into the London slums. Round the corner from Victoria Street is a doss-house, a doorless place, with a stone-flagged corridor, the memory of which "works on his mind like poison". He is haunted by the night-life of the teeming streets, described as strangely and unfamiliarly as though they were in a foreign land: the fights, the atmosphere of suspicion, the houses in which there are faulty drains so that people are dying of typhoid, the thieves, the drunks, the prostitutes: "Look at women; the streets here are a scandal

44

to the world. They won't recognize that they exist—their noses are so damn high! They blink the truth in this middle-class country."

These were the night-time journeys that Galsworthy was making in the first few months after he had moved away from his family home. This was the sort of ferment they were setting up within him, which Harris did not recognize as political. Recalling at the end of his life these night-time wanderings, Galsworthy himself wrote of "communion with the world of dark and broken waters running beneath the bridges of great towns, of shadows passing up and down the alleyways, and enjoying such life as God has given them. . . . I have had my glimpse of another world and tasted the liquors brewed in its dark corners."

At the same time, he was subjected by his sister to the beginnings of what was to be the dominant influence of his whole life and the surge that carried him into his profession as a writer. Lilian and Mabel were deeply concerned about a young woman named Ada who had married a cousin of theirs, Arthur Galsworthy—Major Arthur, as he was later to become —and whose marriage was an unhappy one. Young John had already met Ada Galsworthy at the dinner-party given in honour of her wedding in April 1891, but it was not until he returned from his journeys to Australia and to Russia that he began to learn from his sisters of the depth of her unhappiness. This was at the time when he was trying with the Elstree circle to formulate some sort of philosophical and religious opinions. It was also at the time of the expeditions into the night streets of London slums, and his horror at the hypocrisy with which his own class, his own family—indeed, to some extent, he himself—buttressed their comfortable lives upon the mass wretchedness of the poor. To be shown by his sisters how his own class could equally inflict, in the name of morality, the most desperate misery, as they maintained,

45

upon a young woman who was one of themselves, inflamed in his receptive mind a furious indignation. It was perhaps largely a question of timing. Had he learned of Ada's misery a year or two earlier, while he was still enclosed in a shell of convention, no doubt he would have sympathized, but would privately have considered that there was a lot to be said for the husband's point of view as well. Had he learned of it a few years later, the pity aroused would no doubt have been strong, but his personal philosophy would probably have been sufficiently established to have received it without being greatly involved. Happening as it did in the years when he was making his most intense and desperate efforts to come to terms with existence, it became the dominant fact of his personal life and the basic theme which created the possibility of the novelist.

V

Dr Emanuel Cooper was the leading accoucheur of Norwich in the 1860s and 1870s. The only account of him comes from R. H. Mottram, the novelist, who knew the family well because his father, a Norwich banker, was Dr Cooper's man of business. Mottram described him as a "character", only redeemed from being an oddity by a high professional reputation. His chief delight was to plan and build for himself a classical mausoleum in the Rosary Cemetery at Norwich—the most conspicuous in the graveyard. On Sunday afternoons Dr Cooper used to sit in the cemetery contemplating his mausoleum and smoking a clay pipe. When he died he was found to have appointed a number of noblemen as executors of his will, all of whom declined the honour.

At that time, his two children were in their early teens. The elder was a boy, Arthur Charles, upon whom his mother is said to have doted; the younger a girl, Ada, whom she did not particularly like. Photographs of Ada from childhood into adolescence show a solemn, unsmiling dark-haired child with large, contemplative eyes, growing into a slim young woman with well-formed rather than lovely features, an expression of haughtiness and a firm set of the lips similar to that in the portraits of Galsworthy's mother.

When Dr Cooper laid aside his clay pipe and entered his mausoleum, his wife took the two children away to live at first in Nottingham, later in London. The boy was apprenticed to an engineering works, and her ambition for the girl was to find her a well-to-do husband as soon as possible. She therefore took her to the most fashionable resorts of Europe. They were at Nice during the earthquake which shook their hotel and sent them fleeing back to Paris with the frightened crowd; one terrified woman travelled all the way in a fur coat over her nightdress. They usually wintered in one or other of the great European cities, in Vienna, Florence, Dresden. There they lived hotel lives, and during the day Ada studied the piano, and in the evening as a matter of course they visited the opera. Ada attracted attention because she was a pianist of almost professional skill. In a book of travels which she wrote late in life she somewhat archly recalled a "musical flirtation" which she carried on at Merano with the young Prince Johann of Mecklenburg-Strelitz. They had pianos in adjoining sitting-rooms of the hotel and one would play a theme upon which the other would improvise; she never, however, actually met him. According to Mottram, she received many offers of marriage from very eligible and sometimes titled suitors. These stories, however, were most probably the invention of Mrs Cooper, who would certainly have snatched at a titled marriage. In fact, Ada was well into her twenties before her mother was able to fix a match for her; all the recollections affirm that the marriage was of the mother's arranging. It was not as brilliant as might have been expected.

On one of the journeys abroad—probably at Biarritz, though no exact record of this remains—Mrs Cooper and her daughter Ada met Arthur Galsworthy. He was six years older than Ada, had no profession or occupation (and no intention of taking one), and no money of his own. He lived on an allowance of £700 a year from his father, Frederick Thomas Galsworthy—a younger brother of old John—who was an auctioneer and estate agent of the firm of Chinnock, Galsworthy and Chinnock. Frederick Thomas was also, like all the Galsworthys, a substantial property-owner, and he lived in a large house in Queen's Gate, Kensington. Arthur Galsworthy was a catch only in the sense that one day he would inherit his share of his father's fortune; in fact, since the old man, with Forsyte tenacity, lived until 1917, when he was ninety years of age, the heir chosen as Ada's husband was to wait nearly another thirty years for his inheritance.

Why Ada married him has never been explained. Galsworthy, the novelist, for whom this marriage was to be a torture, makes only a slanting reference to "one or other of the unnumbered reasons for which women marry men, any one of which is good enough until after the event" Ada was certainly not in love with Arthur Galsworthy and they seem to have had no single interest or quality in common. Perhaps she married him simply to get away from her mother or gave in at last in weariness of her mother's persistence. There is a veiled portrait of Mrs Cooper in the character of Mrs Travis in Galsworthy's first novel *Jocelyn*; from the circumstances of the novel it must have been she, though neither Galsworthy nor Ada ever admitted it. "She was frequently heard to say to her niece, 'You ought to think of other people, my dear'. And she did so herself—just so far as it suited her own convenience. . . . She was not really thick-skinned. If people differed or found fault with her she suffered severely until she had time to see that her own view was the right one. She never admitted herself in the wrong. There was no credit due to her for that, she had simply never learned how."

Whatever the reasons for Ada Cooper's marriage to Arthur Galsworthy, it took place in London in April 1891 and was the occasion of several gatherings of the Galsworthy family in full plumage. Ralph Mottram hints that his father, who was then in charge of the Cooper affairs, went to the wedding with misgiving and had been against the match from the start. But Ada was twenty-four years of age; her mother enthusiastically approved; the family of Galsworthys into which she was marrying was of the highest respectability and impressive wealth and although the groom himself commanded only an allowance from his father, Ada's own income from her marriage settlement brought their joint resources to about £1,000 a year. They took a house in South Kensington, near The Boltons, and proceeded to attend dinner-parties given by other branches of the family in Ada's honour, at which she appeared, as the rather charming custom then was, in her wedding dress. After dinner at the Cambridge Gate party she dutifully performed on the piano for her new cousins and accompanied young John in a song. Lilian and Mabel were delighted with her music and her artistic sensibility. The three young women became close friends. Young John saw little of her for a time since he was soon to set off for Australia and then Russia.

It was upon his return that he heard from his sisters that their new cousin Ada's marriage was unhappy, and the nature of that unhappiness.

What was its nature? About that there has been almost complete reticence, coupled with an implication that Arthur Galsworthy was something of a brute.

After the novelist's death, H. V. Marrot assembled the material for his *Life and Letters* under the supervision of Ada herself to whom Galsworthy had, in his will, given complete discretion as to what should or should not appear in a biography. All that Marrot says or was permitted to say is, "Ada Galsworthy's first marriage was a tragic mistake. Blameless and helpless, she was living in extreme unhappiness. Her two loyal friends (Lilian and Mabel) were doing all they could—which was little enough; and from them their brother began to learn—with what distress may be imagined—the torment that married misery can be. It was a very education in pity, and it was to last for many years."

Mottram says in his recollections of Ada that in marrying Arthur Galsworthy she "made a mistake. The bare fact is all that can possibly be important, at the distance of over fifty years."

But the bare fact of this particular mistake is by no means the important aspect of the affair at all. This unhappy marriage and the emotions it aroused in John Galsworthy are the foundation of all his writings. It turned him into the leading novelist of his generation; in particular, it was the direct cause and the very stuff of his first and best Forsyte novel, *The Man of Property*. These happenings created Galsworthy the novelist. Even Marrot admits that "without Ada Galsworthy he might never have become a writer, and without the experience of these years he must, had he written at all, have written very differently".

The account of what was happening in Ada's married life came to Lilian, Mabel and their brother entirely, of course, from Ada herself. None of them left any record of what they were told although Galsworthy transmuted the whole thing into the act of property which Soames Forsyte committed against his wife, Irene—the central incident of the Forsyte story. On the novelist's side of the family there is a continuing image of Arthur Galsworthy as a man addicted to drink, who, in his cups, behaved brutishly. Years later, Ada recounted some stories of her first marriage to Viola Sauter, the wife of Galsworthy's nephew, Rudolf. Rudo and Vi Sauter, as they were always known, lived for a long time with Ada and John Galsworthy after Lilian, Rudo's mother, had died, and were treated almost as though they were their children. It is probable that no woman was ever more in Ada's confidence than was Vi Sauter, and the tales she heard of Arthur Galsworthy were horrifying enough; in more recent times, they would, if true, have been ample for Ada to have obtained a divorce on grounds of cruelty.

From the other side of the family, however, comes a picture of Arthur Galsworthy which does not in the least fit in with any such account. To his second wife—for he married again a few years after he had divorced Ada—he was not at all the sort of person whom Ada described. The second wife, Mrs Wilhelmine Galsworthy, although elderly, was kind enough to furnish some recollections of her husband with whom she lived, she said, very happily for many years until he died and by whom she bore two children.

She strongly disputed any suggestion that her husband could ever have been addicted to drink. In all her years with him she never knew him to drink alcohol during the daytime; in the evening he would usually have one whisky and soda with his dinner and occasionally a glass of port or a liqueur afterwards. This account of his habitual sobriety was confirmed by a housekeeper who was in Mrs Wilhelmine's service while her husband was still alive, and still looking after her.

Mrs Wilhelmine's description of Arthur Galsworthy was of a rather shy, mild and reserved man. He suffered from the feeling that, from his youth onward, his family had always looked upon him as something of a failure. He went to Eton and although he was not sacked from that school his career there was not regarded by his family as a success. When he left school he seems not to have had any wish to go up to a university or, indeed, to do anything much at all. Throughout his life he never worked but lived on the allowance from his father and on the expectation of an inheritance on his father's death. Most of the peacetime years of his second marriage were passed in a simple country life in Somerset; his income was insufficient for anything but a modest house and tastes.

His strongest and abiding interest was the Army or, rather, the Yeomanry, since he was never a Regular soldier. In his young days he served in the Essex Yeomanry and devoted himself assiduously and wholeheartedly to the interests of the volunteer force. He was on active service in South Africa throughout the Boer War and when the First World War broke out he contrived to get himself commissioned again, although by then he was fifty-four years of age. He served part of the time in France, until he suffered a stroke and was invalided out of the Army. He retained in peacetime the rank of Major which he reached during his military years.

He did not often speak with his second wife of his first marriage, but from what he occasionally let slip, Mrs Wilhelmine drew a very different picture of the household in South Kensington. According to what he told her, he and Ada drew apart almost from the start. He was, said his second wife, a man who in the intimacies of marriage was timid and easily rebuffed, and perhaps this was why, as he confided to her, Ada and he were sexually incompatible. He told her that almost from the beginning of his marriage, they were not, as she put it, "on terms". The reason, Mrs Wilhelmine believed, was that, besides their lack of sexual relationship, they found they had nothing in common and on the whole disliked each other. Ada's outstanding interest was music and Arthur could not put up with music for very long. Equally, it was only a short time before Ada was heartily tired of anything to do with the Essex Yeomanry. Any suggestion that Arthur Galsworthy forced his wife to continue a loveless marriage which was torture to her was dismissed by Mrs Wilhelmine as absurd. Arthur simply was not that sort of man at all. He never tried to dominate anybody, he was never offensive and his reaction to any sort of scene or disagreement would be no more than a pained courtesy. Given a basic interest in the Yeomanry—which came perhaps more naturally to Mrs Wilhelmine since she was herself the daughter of a General—she said that Major Arthur was a very easy person to live with, asking little of life except a modest comfort and frequent evenings of bridge, a game at which he was highly skilled. It was Mrs Wilhelmine's opinion that the stories that Ada put about to her intimates of her unhappy married life were the exaggerated imaginings of a somewhat neurotic woman who found that she was bored with the man she had married and was seeking to justify, to herself as well as to her closest friends, her resentment of the fact that he was equally bored with her.

Whether the stories of Ada's sufferings were true, however, or largely imagined, is immaterial. What counts is their effect upon cousin John. In the small enclosed circle of the young Galsworthy women, shuddering with sensitivity, Ada's troubles seemed such a monstrous injustice that their brother, taken in this most vulnerable year of his mental and moral growth, felt first a consuming pity for her, and then fell overwhelmingly and unalterably in love.

VI

Their first meeting after he returned from his journeys abroad was suitably Forsytean, "over pigeon pie at the Eton and Harrow match at Lords in 1893". That is to quote the brief account of the love affair by Marrot, composing the *Life and Letters* soon after Galsworthy died, with the widowed Ada looking over his shoulder. In this passage he was certainly writing to Ada's dictation. The next incident he records occurred on the wedding day, in the summer of 1894, of Lilian Galsworthy and Georg Sauter. When the reception was over, young John walked round to Ada's house in South Kensington and they had a "wistful talk of the much-loved friend and sister they had 'lost' ". They evidently met on many further occasions, though not with Lilian present, for she and her husband had settled for a while in a little Bavarian watering-place, Woerishofen, where they had gone for their honeymoon. They stayed for more than a year, Georg devoting himself to painting. Their son, Rudo, was born there. Soon afterwards they went to Rome. By the time they returned to London, to live for a while with the family at Cambridge Gate, the love affair between Ada and young John was in full progress. Lilian, therefore, certainly had no hand in helping it forward and probably little knowledge of it, though she is known afterwards to have approved of the steps that her brother and her friend took.

When Ada went with her mother for a holiday in Monte Carlo in the Easter of 1895, young John went to Monte Carlo too. It was there that they knew and admitted to each other that they were in love. Ada once told Mottram's mother that the realization came to her during an hotel dinner on the

Riviera and she spoke of the "mingled joy and horror" it brought to her. Galsworthy himself has sufficiently described what occurred, for he used their experiences as a basis for his first novel, *Jocelyn* (admittedly in part autobiographical), and in the central section of a much later novel, the most passionate he wrote, *The Dark Flower*. In the composition of both Ada was, as always, intimately involved. It was together that they set down, in those two books, the essence of their own love affair, substituting for themselves the characters of Giles Legard and Jocelyn Ley in the former and Mark Lennan and Olive Cramier in the latter.

The dangers in culling biography from experiences which a writer has transmuted into a novel are obvious, though they are perhaps less than usual in the case of Galsworthy. He was not a highly imaginative novelist but rather a careful observer who had the patience (and the time) to acquire an immense technical skill. Moreover, the basis of the stories of both these novels is very close to what is known of the story of Ada and John Galsworthy in the days when they fell in love.

It is as Mark Lennan that Galsworthy described how he came to follow Ada to Monte Carlo: "First the merest friendliness, because she was so nice about his work; then respectful admiration, because she was so beautiful; then pity, because she was so unhappy in her marriage. If she had been happy, he would have fled. The knowledge that she had been unhappy long before he met her had kept his conscience quiet. And at last one afternoon she said: 'Ah! if you come out there too!' Marvellously subtle, the way that one little outslipped saying had worked in him, as though it had a life of its own—like a strange bird flown into the garden of his heart, and established with its new song and flutterings, its new flight, its wistful and ever clearer call. That and one moment, a few days later in her London drawing-room, when he had told her that he *was* coming, and she did not, could not, he felt, look at him. Queer! nothing momentous—and yet it had altered all the future!"

At Monte Carlo itself there is the moment of mutual realization that they are in love: "Nothing could take away the look she had given him then. Nothing could ever again separate her from him utterly. She had confessed in it to the same sweet, fearful trouble that he himself was feeling. She had not spoken, but he had seen her lips part, her breast rise and fall. And *he* had not spoken. What was the use of words?"

In both novels there is the man's resolve that whatever he does he must not harm the woman; and her terrified sensation of slipping towards disaster. There are little repeated scenes, such as that of the man standing outside a room in which the woman is playing the piano—a scene that Galsworthy used several times in various places—and "that which was real, the only thing which had substance, was the girl playing that tune in the shuttered room. Nothing else mattered." There is another little scene, which also he several times repeated, of the man standing outside the woman's room at night and seeing her open a window and come out on to the balcony, without her being aware that he is there.

In *Jocelyn* the man's tortured dilemma and the woman's fear are the more fully expressed (and the more clumsily, but, for that reason, perhaps, also the more accurately). For Giles Legard "conventional morality ceased to be anything . . . but a dim shadow falling at times across the path of his loving. He was face to face with two very grim realities, gaunt and shadowless, which hurt him, bit into his soul, absorbed his consciousness—his great unslaked thirst and his dread of bringing her harm." The sense of degradation in Jocelyn's voice when they have admitted their love "wounded him like the cut of a knife": "That expression of shrinking, almost of horror, in her face haunted him; sometimes he would go away cursing himself, calling himself a brute and a beast for bringing her a moment's pain—he would even resolve to give her up and never see her again; but to no end—he could not keep away."

In both novels the woman returns to London in a state of desperation. Olive Cramier realizes as soon as she and her husband are together again that for ever and ever now he is her enemy, "from whom she must guard and keep herself if she could; keep, at all events, each one of her real thoughts and hopes. She could have writhed and cried out." She must force herself to endure his touch, "the full danger to her, and perhaps to Mark himself, of shrinking from this man, striking her with all its pitiable force". When she is left alone in her own room, she stands "without sound or movement, thinking: 'What am I going to do? How am I going to live?'"

Whether or not Ada felt her situation so desperately, she did return from Monte Carlo to Major Arthur's house and continue their life together, such as it was, without giving him any indication of the love that had now been spoken between her and his cousin. So far it had been no more than spoken. All that summer in London the two of them struggled with the question of whether or no to commit adultery. In *Jocelyn* Giles Legard carries for three days a revolver in his pocket: "There was always that escape from the torture of the slowly-moving hours." No doubt that was an exaggeration of Galsworthy's own feelings, though in these early days of his love there seems always to have been a death-wish hidden. Olive Cramier is drowned immediately after she has at last given herself to Mark Lennan; to achieve the pinnacle of love and then immediately to pay the penalty of death, that was the ideal. But such noble sentiments remained merely sentiments. They did not, that summer, suffer even the lesser death of parting. "They were soon meeting as often as possible," wrote Marrot, on Ada's authority, "and he read her his stories as they came to him. . . . Then, in September of 1895, they became lovers, and there began the long turmoil of their hearts—that life 'spun between ecstasy and torture' which was to last through nine mortal years."

It would seem, by a brief and discreet note of journeys that Ada left behind, that they became lovers at Yarmouth, in Norfolk. Of how they came to be there together there is now no record.

By then they had the second bond between them that he had begun to write. He himself has said that he did so at Ada's instigation, and that he would never have thought of attempting the task had it not been for something she said to him, a chance remark, in the Gare du Nord at Paris, where he was seeing her and her mother off during that visit to Monte Carlo in the Easter of 1895; it must have been on the return journey, so that they were still in the dazedly happy state of having declared their love for each other, without having properly faced the problems that were still a few hours ahead in London.

According to Galsworthy's own account written at the very end of his life of this incident at the Gare du Nord, he and Ada were standing by a bookstall in the station and she murmured to him, "You are just the person to write, why don't you?" This remark aroused in him the determination to begin a career as a writer which previously he had not considered. But it is far more probable that, in his recollection after the passage of years, and when all the writing was done, he sentimentally, perhaps by then unknowingly, exaggerated Ada's part in order to please her, to add one more gift to the many he had given her throughout their life together. It was a gift that she, of course, accepted; writing after Galsworthy's death, she also claimed it was her remark "which gave the first impetus towards the literary calling of John Galsworthy". But in fact this was not the first time he had thought of writing as a career; he had already discussed it some six months earlier in a letter to Monica Sanderson. The idea had certainly been in his mind—"I do wish I had the gift of writing. I really think that it is the nicest way of making money going." He disliked being dependent on his father's bounty. He disliked the legal career upon which he had so desultorily and unsuccessfully begun. He detested that part of his father's property business which had introduced to him the unwelcome knowledge of the slum houses from which some of the rents came. He wanted to break away from all this, change his life before he got into the routine of working for the sake of an income. But how? He knew nothing else, and had no alternative ambition, except, perhaps, to earn enough to live on by practising some sort of art, as his new brother-in-law contrived to do. That would be a worthy, worthwhile way of spending a life. Alas, he could not paint, he was not musical. If only, as once before he had sighed, he had the gift of writing. As they came back from Monte Carlo, there was this added burden of joy and terror placed upon his life. He must have been thinking with a mixture of exaltation and despair of what his future could be. Must they part, and he return for ever to the dreariness of Law and the guiltiness of money? Or was there the wildest, most unlikely chance, that he could launch himself into a new life, with Art as the exalted aim and with freedom from the narrow conventions that would otherwise separate them? Ah, if only he had the gift of writing. Then she murmured, "But you are just the person to write. Why don't you?"

It is far more likely that Ada's remark occurred in some such way as that, as part of a long and tortured discussion of the future, rather than as a sudden idea with nothing leading up to it. This, of course, diminishes the image Galsworthy wanted to create for her as his sole inspiration. She simply expressed, at precisely the right moment, a word of encouragement that made possible to his imagination an ambition he had been hesitantly cherishing but had not had the courage to accept. Even so, she showed a remarkable percipience. This was not merely a chance remark made because she thought it was what he wanted to hear, for she followed it up. Galsworthy's original impulse to write may not have come solely from her, but it is to her and her alone that he owed the fact that two years later he was still trying to do so. He began by writing short stories which he imagined were in the manner of Bret Harte or after the style of Rudyard Kipling. Even these did not dismay Ada as, one by one, he brought them round for her opinion. A woman as sensitive as she to anything artistic cannot but have seen that the stories were for the most part inept, painfully amateur, shallow and false. Nevertheless she kept him to his new task. Without the slightest evidence upon which to base the belief, she seems to have been quite assured that, with perseverance, he would become a notable writer. It is as though the closeness with which they were now to interweave their lives and their thoughts had already given her an intuitive understanding of a mental power and capacity within him of which he himself was still unaware and of which, certainly, for some couple of years at least, he showed very little sign.

VII

He began his first short story in his little narrow room, his chambers at No. 3 Paper Buildings, in the Inner Temple. It was called "Dick Denver's Idea", and is about an American gambler on a journey in the Far East who rids a woman of a brute of a husband by killing him in a duel in a cave in which a geyser spouts conveniently to dispose of the corpse; Dick Denver, being at heart an honourable man, does not then try to take advantage of the woman. This completely implausible melodrama contains in an oddly distorted way several of the strands of Galsworthy himself. Dick Denver is a gambler; he lives, that is, without depending on any conventional work for a source of income. The woman is unhappily married—so unhappily that the husband deserves to die—and Dick has the coolness of nerve to kill him without acting dishonourably (the duel), and without the slightest risk of penalty (the geyser). The setting of the story comes, of course, from Galsworthy's own journey to the Pacific. Finally, Dick Denver nobly renounces the woman for whom he has done so much, as Galsworthy must often have wished, as he wrote, that he could as truly and honourably renounce Ada in spite of the passion which was thrusting him towards her.

When he read the story to Ada, she encouraged him. He therefore began another, then another. To the task of writing, rewriting and revising short stories he devoted the next two years of his life. Most of them were as amateur and improbable as "Dick Denver's Idea". Several of them derive from the Pacific journey. One, "The Doldrums", is an attempt to model a character upon Conrad, and another, "Ashes", sounds like a story that Conrad had casually told him but did not want to use. Those set in far places have such titles as "The Running Amok of Synge Sahib" and "The Capitulation of Jean Jacques" and are grossly sentimental. Two are set in London and are Galsworthy's first attempts to portray the city of St James's, the clubs and Kensington which he was to make peculiarly his. In one, called "Tally-ho—Budmash", a sentimental General takes to his club a five-year-old boy, son of a gunner in India, who has been lost by his *sais* in St James's Park. The child talks in a dreadful phonetic travesty of children's speech and the whole thing is so deplorable that admiration at Ada's ability to see here a future writer rises to pure astonishment.

Among the ten stories, however, was one, "The Demi-Gods", in which for the first time Galsworthy began to feel his touch. The reason is that this was the first time he ventured to transmute into fiction the affair between Ada and himself. Directly he touched that theme most of the falseness fell away and even the quality of the prose itself somewhat improved. A young couple, at the end of a stolen month together by an Italian lake, must tomorrow return to London, "back to prison—to prison—to prison. The thought beat through both hearts, with the level monotony of a tolling for the dead, for the glorious dead, for the month past of a sweet and lovely life together in the garden of rest. Tomorrow was the ending of all life and light, bringing with it for her a separation from the true self, a return behind the triumphant car of a mocking and over-riding fate, to a caged existence, a loathed companionship, a weary, weary beating of the breast against the bars; for him—a legion of mind-devils, torturing, twisting, lying in wait at every turn and corner of life, ever alert and ever cruel, and a dreary, craving ache."

The young couple are to have one last day of happiness in the mountains, in a hired carriage driven by an old Italian who throughout the day takes too much to drink. Absorbed in their last paradisal day, they do not notice this, even when on the way home the driver nods off to sleep. Across the lake stretch railway and road bridges side by side. The horse shies on to the single-track railway bridge, the driver is thrown off and the girl flings her arms around her lover, holding them both in the carriage to meet, in collision with the oncoming train, death at their rapturous day's end.

This was Ada and John's own situation and this the death-wish that haunted the early days of their love, in all its furtiveness. Her meetings with young John in London were at one or other of the little studios that he successively took; for by now, of course, he needed to set up separate house. He lived for a time at 2 Cedar Studios in Glebe Place, South Kensington; then at 4 Lawrence Mansions on Chelsea Embankment; and at last in a studio at 16A Aubrey Walk, off Campden Hill. This was in a mews above a stable (the stableman's wife catered for him), overlooking the reservoir that adjoins Holland Park. Mottram, who visited him there, recalls that he slept on a camp bed under rugs made from the skins of animals he had shot on his travels and that in one corner of the studio was one of the "new patent Turkish bath cabinets, for he was already then beginning to feel the rheumatism which was one of the ills of his later years".

Besides these meetings in London, Galsworthy and Ada contrived to go abroad together at least once every year, and usually to spend some time together somewhere in England during the summer. Ada left a list of these journeys, which were extensive. In 1896 they spent Easter at Lucerne, Lugano, Genoa and Monte Carlo. In the summer they were together at Edinburgh and York. The following Easter they were around the Italian lakes with once again a trip to Monte Carlo; in the summer they met at Hunstanton in England and also toured down the Rhine; and at some time in the winter they were together at Torquay. So it went on. Each Easter there was a journey to Italy, Switzerland and the south of France and every summer a holiday together in England—usually in Devon and Cornwall—and as often as not a visit to Germany; and twice they managed to get away to Torquay in the winter.

What is surprising is that these journeys, as well as the London meetings, were all carried on secretly. Marrot refers to a woman relative who, as chaperon, "presented to them a resolute blind eye", but travelled everywhere with them. There is now no record of who this could have been; the only likely candidate seems to be Mrs Cooper but the whole thing sounds improbable. Lilian and Mabel knew what was happening and Ada once told Vi Sauter that the travels were made a lot easier, even in the days when passports were not required, by the fact that she was already a Mrs Galsworthy. But how was it all hidden from Major Arthur? His second wife was quite sure from what he told her of his marriage to Ada, that while she was living in his house he had no idea that she was conducting an affair with his cousin. The London meetings were possible, it seems, because of the closely-mingled life of all the branches of the Galsworthy family. They were always popping in and out of each other's homes and when Ada was away for an afternoon, Major Arthur never suspected infidelity but assumed that she had called in to see Lilian or to spend an hour or two playing the piano with Mabel. It seems probable that he was by then insufficiently interested in his wife to bother to inquire much about her activities. The affairs of the Essex Yeomanry took a great deal of his time and he frequently went off to Colchester to take part in them. No doubt, too, there were training courses to attend and camps to be kept. At such times he was quite content to let his wife set off on a holiday abroad: she had always toured a great deal on the continent and would come to no harm. Perhaps it was to allay any disquiet he may have felt that the mysterious chaperon was employed. What is certain is that the journeys were contrived. A few years later, when the Boer War broke out, things became easier still. Major Arthur sailed at once for South Africa and Ada's coast was clear.

The question as to why they kept their love affair secret is harder to answer. They intended, after the first few months, eventually to get Major Arthur to divorce her, so that John could marry her. There were no children involved. Why, then, should they wait through dragging years of secrecy and torment? Why not have the scandal straight away, since they were to have it in the end?

The explanation that Ada gave to Marrot after Galsworthy's death was that, although concealment was repugnant to both of them, "what of the old man, his father? Absorbed though they were in each other, he must not, should not be forgotten. He was seventy-eight years old, and a Victorian of the Victorians in many ways, for all his bigness of soul; could he be expected to accept with composure that which training and the habit of years must force him to regard as a scandal? If it be objected, on the one hand, that the sacrifice was too great, their conscientiousness exaggerated, or, on the other, that her husband was the first person to be considered, the answer comes, firstly, that the circumstances fully—even amply— entitled Ada Galsworthy to take her happiness where she could find it, and secondly, that they are seldom if ever wrong, who choose, as these two did, the unselfish course. At any rate, 'Neither', wrote one of them, 'would contemplate for one moment doing anything that could grieve the very declining years of his father, to whom they were both utterly devoted; and so they went on—furtive but never ashamed, agonized but deliriously happy, meeting on edge, parting in dejection; she always ready to lie down and die, he always ready to outface the devil and destruction.' "

This explanation, besides being a little high-minded, does

omit some relevant facts. One is that old John, Victorian though he might have been, was not quite so sensitive to scandal as is implied. When his younger son, Hubert, got himself threatened with a breach of promise action in South Africa, he paid up the £500 necessary to get him out of that scrape without unusual perturbation; and it was not to be long before his own wife was to leave him, on the grounds that she suspected him of too great a familiarity with his grandson's governess.

The other fact which is not mentioned is the almost complete dependence of young John on the income his father allowed him. It was all he had and all that, for a long time ahead, he had any prospect of getting. Ada had an income from her marriage allowance but it was far too small to keep them both. If old John's reaction to a threatened scandal had been to declare that either the liaison must cease or the allowance would, there is no begging the fact that Galsworthy's whole life would have been overthrown. Among other things, he would have had to give up the attempt to make authorship his career. He has often been depicted as a young man who could afford to write in the security of his wealth. That is not so. His income, though not large, was sufficient for his needs so long as it continued but it was by no means guaranteed. His father could have cut it off at any time; and not only the income. If old John had ordered his son to put an end to the affair and his son had refused to obey him, there was nothing to prevent his cutting him out of his very substantial will.

Those who knew Galsworthy most intimately in later years, particularly his nephew Rudo, are quite sure that he would never have allowed such considerations to weigh at all in deciding to keep his love affair secret. Rudo Sauter adds, indeed, that his grandfather, old John, would never in any case have penalized his son financially for following where his heart led. The only slight evidence there is, however, goes the other way. In his will, old John was markedly less generous to his son Hubert than to his son John. Hubert's own son has always understood that this was a penalty for his father's youthful indiscretion in South Africa.

Certainly Major Arthur, on the evidence of what he told his second wife, had no doubt at all, when he discovered what was going on, that young John and Ada were keeping the matter quiet solely because they feared the loss of the allowance. But then, he could hardly have been expected to take a very lofty view of his cousin's principles.

VIII

The story now concentrates into the London borough of
Kensington.

When Georg and Lilian Sauter returned from Rome with
their infant Rudo, they stayed for a time with her parents
in Cambridge Gate. Then old John bought them a house at
1 Holland Park Avenue and converted the upper part into an
enormous studio in which Georg could practise his art and
Lilian live the social and artistic life of a painter's wife; Mottram, who visited them there, recalls that the studio tea-table
was dominated by a Russian samovar covered by a special
straw-woven cosy.

Lilian, with her intensity, her sensitive intellect and her
consuming desire to be a poet, devoted herself, perhaps without too much discrimination, to contemporary art, particularly
to literature. After Ada herself, it was she who earnestly
nurtured her brother's early attempts at authorship and when
he was most amateur may then most have loved him. Georg,
her husband, was nothing of the kind. He was a professional
painter of portraits (and occasionally of landscapes) who
worked hard and achieved a reasonable success. He also played
a useful part in the organization of his profession and was
one of the active founders of the International Society for
Sculptors, Painters and Gravers of which, at various times,
Whistler and Rodin were presidents. The period immediately
following his return from Rome, however, was not his best.
He had fallen too much under Italian influence and his
painting of Lilian and Rudo at this time is marred by
the rich sentimentality implied in the title, "Maternity".
What it does incidentally show is how tiny in stature Lilian

69

was, even in comparison with the child; she weighed only six stone.

In 1897 Mabel, the younger sister, married and settled down in the same district, at 10 Tor Gardens, just off the other side of Campden Hill. Her husband was an engineer named Thomas Blair Reynolds, to whom old John gradually passed over all his directorships, probably because there was nobody else in the family ready to take them on. Although his elder son retained for a time his seats on the boards of some of old John's companies, he was abandoning the Law and had turned to the writing as an occupation (old John can scarcely have thought of it as a career). His younger son, Hubert, had proved something of a wanderer, uninterested in commerce and the City of London. His senior son-in-law was a Bavarian portrait painter, so the only steadfast one remaining was Tom Reynolds, the engineer. There must have been times when old John contemplated with disquiet the male members of this family of a wealthy, self-made businessman. For Tom Reynolds would probably not have been his ideal choice to carry on his business interests. Georg Sauter's portrait of his brother-in-law—he painted them all—shows a man with a noble, rather simple face, drooping moustache, and prominent Adam's apple. One could imagine him as a somewhat visionary engineer, but the City rig of black coat and stiff collar looked rather odd on him. He was not, in fact, particularly suited to the life of commerce. Tom Reynolds was known in the City as an absolutely honourable and upright man—characteristics, as one of the next generation of the family wryly remarked, that do not always lend themselves to the retention of money. He engaged with great ardour in a number of enterprises which did not turn out too well, such projects as the dredging of Russian harbours. There is also a recollection that he was unhappily involved in some gold or copper mine in Africa, the richness of which had been overvalued, not to say salted. In spite of mishaps of this kind, however, his family life with Mabel and their two children was a happy one.

The house in Tor Gardens in which the Reynoldses lived had once been Holman Hunt's, and it already contained the huge studio in the upper parts without which neither of the Galsworthy girls could be really happy. In Mabel's studio were two grand pianos. To it flocked composers and instrumentalists, doubly welcome if they happened to be down on their luck or if their future masterpieces had not yet been recognized or, perhaps, not yet even written. Mabel was intensely musical and intensely warm-hearted. Her sympathies flew out to anybody of a musical nature who needed succour and she would hand out money unstintingly to any lame duck of that kind. Not that all her protégés were lame ducks: two young pianists who worked assiduously in the studio at 10 Tor Gardens were Myra Hess and Harriet Cohen.

Both these Kensington houses—the one redolent of paint, turpentine and the fragrance of the samovar, the other ringing with piano music—were of course fully available to young John whenever he wanted to use them. They opened for him all the young artistic life of social London—the *nouvelle vague*, as it were, of the *fin de siècle*; he seems always to have gazed upon it with a satiric eye behind his monocle. Soon a third house in the same borough was also to be established for his use. Since all the family, save Hubert, were now set up in Kensington, old John and Blanche moved out of Cambridge Gate and in 1898 bought South House, on Campden Hill. They lived there until their quarrel over the governess and their parting, some five years later.

In this setting young John, embellished at this time with a heavy moustache, conducted his private life as discreetly as he could and turned full-time author. He had then written only a few of the short stories that were to be his beginning and nobody except Ada, and possibly Lilian, could have thought the intention anything but the time-passing whim of an idle young man. The directorships in his father's companies which he for a time retained did not, of course, demand any great exertions. As for the law, he spent much of 1896 persuading his parents to allow him to drop it. Although he was approaching his thirtieth year, their consent was necessary, since he was still dependent on his father's generosity. There is no doubt that old John and Blanche Galsworthy had not the slightest expectation of their son's success as a man of letters, nor did they wish for it. When Georg Sauter was painting Blanche's portrait she confided to him during the sittings that she strongly disliked the idea of a son of hers being an author and would dislike it even if he should become a famous one.

Author, however, he now was. His dearest wish, therefore, was naturally to have a book published. All he had to offer were his ten short stories which he put together into a book-length collection under the title *From the Four Winds*, and which he signed by a pseudonym, John Sinjohn. He was unable to find a publisher prepared to put the book out as a venture, so he offered to pay the cost of publication himself and on these terms Fisher Unwin was ready to publish an edition of five hundred copies. When this had been agreed, Galsworthy ventured for the first time to tell his one literary friend, Conrad, that he had taken up writing. Conrad, not having seen the stories themselves, sent a good-natured note to Unwin, commending the new writer as "a first-rate fellow, clever, has seen the world".

In 1897, therefore, *From the Four Winds* was published and duly received notice in the columns of book criticism of the day. Most of the notices were amiable and one or two critics, with a percipience that is admirable but baffling, thought the writer might have a literary future. Galsworthy himself, in later years, had no illusions about the merit of the first volume of stories he published. "That dreadful little book" he called it and withdrew it from circulation. But he admitted that, at the time, it had aroused in him a greater feeling of pride than any subsequent book was able to stir up. It was the easiest thing in the world to forget that it had been published only because he had paid for it. It was possible, though not quite so easy, to be reconciled to the hard fact that almost nobody bought it; a quarter of a century later the publisher still had twenty unsold copies of *From the Four Winds*. But in 1897 none of this mattered. He was an author with one book published and a second being written, this time a novel.

This was *Jocelyn*, the earlier of the two novels in which, as has been seen, he drew for material upon the story of Ada and himself at Monte Carlo. As a novel it is a poor thing. Galsworthy, looking back on it nearly thirty years later, claimed that in *Jocelyn* he was conscious of a feeling for character and a sense of atmosphere but admitted, "it was a bad novel; it was not what is called 'written'. The technique limped; the structure had a stringhalt; and the clothing sentences were redundant or deficient."

What *Jocelyn* does show is how he was groping towards his theme. Galsworthy understood that he was not a born writer and that he could become one only by hard work, infinite pains in revision and rewriting, and concentration upon technique. He acknowledged this in the essay just quoted and added that, although a man who is determined to write and has the grit to see the thing through can get there in time, he does need an independent income or another job while he is learning. This of course he had—and was not going to risk on any account.

He did not perceive so clearly, however, how dependent all his early writing was on his relationship with Ada and he seemed to be impelled almost against his will towards treating of that subject. Yet the closer he drew to the theme of protest at society's cruelty to a woman who has broken out of an unhappy marriage, the more vividly his writing flared. In successive books he turned suddenly to this theme, often with very little relevance to the story he was telling, increasing at each attempt the firmness with which he dared to deal with it and gaining with each increase a greater power; until, in *The Man of Property*, he wrote a book with this as its central theme, and achieved his masterpiece. Afterwards the continuing impulse was sufficient to carry him through a set of three more novels, criticizing late Victorian and Edwardian society in all its aspects, and to die out in a fourth, as the Great War swept away the world which he had attacked because it had regarded Ada with contempt. Only when all this was long past could he discover, in searching for an alternative emotional impulse, what strength could be drawn from a recollection of his relationships with his parents.

In *Jocelyn* he was only groping in the direction of drawing on his own emotional experience. It was necessarily written with Ada's consent and indeed with her aid. As they drifted from meeting to meeting in their hidden life in Kensington, he read to her every line and she criticized and discussed. There are some long passages, in which Jocelyn describes her feelings about the guilty business, that must certainly have been inspired by Ada; one feels they were virtually dictated by her. They were her own feelings as she told them to her lover, even if, for his ear, they were romanticized.

What they both jibbed at, however, was the possibility of identification if Jocelyn were shown as an unhappily married woman. The novel, therefore, is about a love affair between an unmarried girl and an unhappily married man. The plot is improbable and conventionally melodramatic. The girl, Jocelyn, gives herself in a moment of passion to the man, Giles Legard. He later finds his wife, Irma, an invalid, lying unconscious after having accidentally taken an overdose of her sleeping mixture, and leaves her to die. The shadow of the dead woman then separates him from Jocelyn, until, after many miseries, they come together again in a happy ending.

The two settings of the book—the district around Monte Carlo and Mentone, and Chelsea—are sketched in with a hand that was becoming slightly more adroit. Much of the writing is still clumsy, and the strong passages are badly overwritten, but they are given some sort of glow by the intensity of his own feelings which he was trying to express, but could not as yet transmute. "In return for an hour of mad, intoxicating passion he had bartered everything . . . there was not a shred left to him of his honour, his self respect; that didn't seem to matter, he was beyond feeling it. But in the single hour of madness he had taken the happiness of the woman he loved—and with it his own—taken it, as it were, in his two hands and flung it into the dust. Taken her wellbeing, her reserve and her pride and flung them into the dust."

To relieve all this there were the first mere hints of the vein of irony, of comic character, which he was to develop into the portrait of the Forsytes. His first little sketch of this kind is of Jocelyn's aunt, Mrs Travis (whom he must certainly have modelled, as has been noted, on Ada's mother, Mrs Cooper). The best instance is a tiny scene in the Chelsea flat to which Mrs Travis and her niece have returned from Mentone. In her agony, Jocelyn "gave herself up to music, working from morning until night at Brahms, Schumann, Chopin or Bach, to the great discomfort of her aunt, who fidgeted in her seat at Brahms and Chopin, wellnigh howled at Bach, and would plaintively murmur requests for 'The Bees' Wedding' upon which she had been brought up". (One is permitted, perhaps, a moment of sneaking sympathy for Major Arthur, who could console himself, through all this, only with private military thoughts.)

Galsworthy, having finished this novel by the end of 1897, had gained enough confidence to show the manuscript to Conrad, to get an opinion and to seek advice. This habit of consulting his literary friends over a manuscript and suffering agonies of indecision, followed by months of rewriting, on their advice, was one that he was soon to develop strongly. Of all of them, he must best have liked showing manuscripts to Conrad, who usually lavished upon them quite extravagant praise. They were by now firm friends. Galsworthy was helping Conrad financially, and it is difficult to avoid detecting hypocrisy in the latter's response to a reading of the earlier manuscripts. Of *Jocelyn*, for example, he wrote, "The merit of the book (apart from distinguished literary expression) is just in this: you have given the exact measure of your characters in a language of great felicity, with measure, with poetical appropriateness, to characters tragic indeed but within the bounds of their nature. That's what makes the book valuable apart from its many qualities as a piece of literary work. In fact the force of the book is in its fidelity to the surface of life—to the surface of events—to the surface of things and ideas. Now this is not being shallow . . . the achievement is as praiseworthy as though you had plumbed the very ocean. It is not your business to invent depths—to invent depths is not art either. Most things and most natures have nothing but a surface. A fairly prosperous man in the state of modern society is without depth—but he is complicated—just in the way you show him. I don't suppose you admire such beings any more than I do. Your book is a passionate analysis of high-minded and contemptible types—and you awaken sympathy, interest, feeling in an impartial, artistic way. It is an achievement."

To a relative in Poland, Conrad wrote, "The novel is not remarkable, but the man is very pleasant and kind."

Encouraged, no doubt, by the opinion of his friend, at the

end of January 1898 Galsworthy sent off the manuscript to Fisher Unwin, suggesting the terms that Conrad had proposed he should ask—the author to receive 5d. per copy up to 500 copies; 10d. 500-2000; after that 1s. per copy. Within a fortnight he received the somewhat galling reply that Unwin could not see his way to "venturing" the book, but would be prepared to publish it on the same terms as the previous one, namely, at the author's expense. Galsworthy, nettled, refused this offer, but said he would be very glad to have Unwin's view and criticism of the work. In his reply, Unwin quoted a sentence from his reader's report, "the author is essentially a clubman". This stung badly. Writing more than thirty years later, Galsworthy was still protesting irritably about it. He was not a clubman. For him, a club was simply a place where he hung his hat and weighed himself. In all his life he had not made more than a dozen acquaintances in a club, and not one single friend. The publisher's reader had been deceived by the simple fact that he had written to Unwin on Junior Carlton Club notepaper. And so he fumed on. No clubman, he.

This publisher's reader was in fact Edward Garnett, the critic who discovered, encouraged and taught their early lessons to so many men who were to become writers destined for distinction, at the cost of never having time to write the distinguished books of which he continually felt himself to be capable. He was later to become an invaluable, tireless teacher to Galsworthy himself; but he was never truly to be forgiven that "clubman" jibe.

Galsworthy did at last find a publisher, Gerald Duckworth, who would put out the novel at his own expense and it was published in 1898 under the same pseudonym of John Sinjohn. It was neither well received nor a success. Most critics who troubled to review it disliked it. Only the *Saturday Review* had the understanding to comment, "Mr Sinjohn, on the whole, puts some life into his stale materials; he observes, he has insight, humour. If he were only content to dispense with a plot, we can imagine him achieving something quite respectable in fiction."

IX

The terms which Duckworth had offered him were "a deferred royalty", which in the event yielded him nothing, though at least *Jocelyn* cost him nothing. He was at this point feeling discouraged. His chosen career, after nearly four years, had yielded him neither profit nor acclaim and he reckoned that, apart from incidental expenses, it had cost him a hundred pounds—spent, of course, on the publication of the volume of short stories. Conrad was still trying to sustain his ambition by letters in which kindness is more evident than sincerity and by showing his work to his own literary friends, Garnett and Ford Madox Hueffer. He sent Galsworthy every bud of comfort he could pluck—"Hueffer fell in love with *The Four Winds*", etc. But it was not, according to Galsworthy himself, the encouragement of others that persuaded him to persevere, but the inspiration of de Maupassant and Turgeniev, whose work he now began to read intensively. Of the two, it was Turgeniev, as Constance Garnett had then translated his novels, who most influenced him—"*the* man above all others I should like to have known," he once said. What he got from them apart from aesthetic excitement, was "an insight into proportion of theme and economy of words", an inspiration of technique.

He began, in consequence, his second novel, *Villa Rubein*. He knew by now that he must choose a theme from his own experience, but he had said all that, at that time, he dared say about himself and Ada. For *Villa Rubein*, therefore, he turned to the event which had earlier disturbed and questioned the conventional upbringing and had first introduced him to the life ambitions and ideals of an artist. He turned to the upheaval caused in Cambridge Gate when his sisters brought home the young Bavarian painter, Georg Sauter. *Villa Rubein*, which he dedicated to Lilian, is the love story of a young Austrian painter, Alois Harz, and a gentle, rather noble English girl, Christian Devorell. The setting is not England, but the Austrian Tyrol; the Villa Rubein is at Botzen (Bolzano). The girl is in the care of two old men, her English uncle, Nicholas Treffry, and her Czech stepfather, Herr Paul, both of whom disapprove of a match between her and the young painter. Herr Paul, discovering that Harz, years before, had escaped from arrest for a youthful Anarchist escapade, betrays him to the police. Treffry, learning of this in time, takes the young man on a perilous drive over the mountains and across the Italian border to safety; but the rigours of the drive bring on the illness of which Treffry is to die. This parts the lovers; although even this is insufficient to prevent the happy ending which Galsworthy quite gratuitously stuck on to the end of the tale—Harz and Christian married three years later and established with their child in a comfortable studio in London.

Leaving aside the melodrama, this is of course the story of Georg Sauter's love for Lilian and its effect upon old John Galsworthy; there is a languid aunt, Mrs Decie, who in her civilized and ineffectual disapproval of the proposed match owes something to Blanche. Its theme is that of conflict between the life of art and of money. Treffry, a first attempt at depicting the London men of business who were to be developed into the Forsytes—Treffry lives on in old Jolyon's memory as his partner in a firm of City tea-merchants—is a man who has been brought up in the power and respect of money. He is kindly, and of a just and generous nature, and on those terms he and Harz can meet each other's minds. But always there is between them the barrier, on his side, of the importance of money; and, on the painter's side, of the ruthless devotion to art. "You know as much of art as I know of money," says Harz to Treffry at the height of their conflict; "If we live a thousand years we shall never understand each other."

This conflict and the characters of Harz and Christian all came from Sauter's marriage to Lilian. But beneath the surface theme, Galsworthy was also starting to work, clumsily and without having grasped it fully, at the conflict between the free spirit and the conventional world over the soul of a woman. In this sense, *Villa Rubein* was not about Georg and Lilian at all, but about himself and Ada. He was separated from her by the conventions of middle-class England; by her marriage, to dissolve which would mean infinite pain and shame for her; and by not daring to face old John, whether for noble reasons of respect for his feelings or whether for less noble fears for the allowance from his purse. Although Georg and Lilian Sauter's marriage was disapproved by the family, there were no such agonies and moral conflicts for them to endure as Harz and Christian suffer in *Villa Rubein*. The torments of the book, badly expressed though as yet they are, were the torments of young Galsworthy in the furtive affair he was conducting with his cousin's wife in Kensington, although their every meeting conflicted harshly with the principles in which he had been brought up and which remained basically strong in him, for all his attempts to replace them with the freedom of the artist. At one point in the book the circumstances of his own affair burst through. At dinner at the Villa Rubein when the women have retired, Herr Paul suddenly recounts a piece of scandal, of a woman who has run off from her husband, and his determination to get her back. This, of course, is the situation that Galsworthy and Ada were ever contemplating for themselves; the long passage in the novel is an irrelevancy and a blemish. There is no purpose to it, except to allow Galsworthy to argue, through his characters—but quite out of their character—that to "make a woman live with you, if she don't want to? I call it low"; that "the marriage tie is the biggest thing there is! But, by Jove, I'm a Dutchman if hunting women ever helped the marriage tie"; that as to honour, "if huntin' women's your idea of honour, well—it isn't mine. . . . Forgiveness is another thing. I leave that to your sanctimonious beggars. But, hunt a woman! Hang it, sir, I'm not a cad! This is a subject that don't bear talking of."

Villa Rubein is the first of Galsworthy's narratives to begin to show his skill. When he came to sum up his work, he considered it "more genuine, more atmospheric, better balanced, but still it was not 'written' ". He tried to remedy this when it was reissued by Duckworth, bound up with some short stories, seven years afterwards. He then thoroughly revised it twice over, until the narrative, at least, seemed to him sufficiently direct and limpid; he never attempted to remedy its structural defects. What it does have is a youthful freshness, concise scenic settings and dialogue pared down, in the fashion of the two masters upon whom he was modelling himself, with an abrupt economy of words; particularly it has a successful portrait of an elderly man of affairs, at which he was always to excel. Nicholas Treffry is alive in the same way that old Jolyon was to come to life and probably for the same reason—the childhood devotion of Galsworthy to his father that persisted throughout his life.

When *Villa Rubein* was published by Duckworth in the autumn of 1900, once again under the pseudonym of John Sinjohn, it largely went unnoticed. But it was received with fair appreciation by the few writers and literary men to whom Galsworthy was then being introduced by Conrad and to whom he ventured to send copies. One of them, H. G. Wells, wrote in reply a polite note about the finely-drawn figures, especially of the older men, though he permitted himself an ironic doubt as to the existence of the "Artistic Temperament", which the book was all about. Hueffer, at enormous length, was at first flowery and then obliging enough to describe how he would have treated the novel had it been his own work. Like his previous book, it earned the writer not a penny in its original edition. But this no longer irked him even slightly. His course, he was convinced, was now set. Major Arthur was away at the Boer War. Galsworthy and Ada had clearly determined now that their lives must run together. He was equally determined that his task in life was to write and to this he applied himself, though with scant encouragement except from the loyal Conrad who was even beginning to feel that his young friend might be able to make something of letters after all. To Mabel, whom he had got to know well in earlier years at the Sandersons', Conrad wrote that it was "a wonderful example of what a determined singleness of purpose can achieve when there is a solid basis of a remarkable talent that I verily believe will go very far— practically as far as he chooses to push it". Recognition, he declared, would come, though it was unlikely—though not impossible—that her brother would ever be able to look forward to other than limited appreciation.

His next volume, *A Man of Devon*, was the last he published under his pseudonym. It is a collection of four long-short stories which he began to write a few weeks before *Villa Rubein* was published, and completed in the following year. They are all about infatuation. In the title story it is the infatuation of a Devon farmer's daughter for a buccaneer; in "Silence", the least successful of the four, of a mine manager in a remote province of Canada for power; in "A Knight", which sprang from an old man whom Galsworthy and Ada met on one of their trips to the South of France, the infatuation of a man for his unfaithful wife despite her infidelity. In the fourth story, "The Salvation of Swithin Forsyte", it is that Forsyte uncle's infatuation as a young man, recalled on his deathbed, for a daughter of a wild family of Hungarian exiles for whose sake he nearly gets embroiled in an absurd revolutionary incident. But at almost the point where it would become impossible to draw back, Forsyte caution reasserts itself: "He was visited by a horrible suspicion. When he could bear it no longer, he started up in bed. What if it were all a plot to get him to marry her? . . . He seated himself on the bed, holding his head in his hands, solemnly thinking out what such a marriage meant. In the first place it meant ridicule, in the next place ridicule, and in the last place ridicule. She would eat chicken bones with her fingers—those fingers his lips still burned to kiss. She would dance wildly with other men. She would talk of her 'dear Father-town', and all the time her eyes would look beyond him, somewhere or other into some d—d place he knew nothing of. He sprang up and paced the room, and for a moment thought he would go mad." He walks out of the inn at which they are all lodging, tramps the woods in despair and, on coming back to find the girl smiling from her window at him, is seized with an inexplicable terror, jumps into his carriage and flees back to Salzburg. There he rejoins his brother, James, who simply grunts, "You don't look the thing." Swithin does not, indeed, recover from his daze until after he and James have taken homeward ship from Genoa: "Only then did he show signs of any healthy interest in life, when, finding that a man on board was perpetually strumming, he locked the piano up and pitched the key into the sea." And only one faint lingering echo of his infatuation remains (until he recalls it with a muttered, "I've missed it" on his deathbed); this is when a girl coming from a side-street into Piccadilly accosts him in German: "Swithin, after staring at her in silence for some seconds, handed her a five-pound note, to the great amazement of his friend; nor could he himself have explained the meaning of this freak of generosity."

Mottram, who regards this volume of short stories as "Jack's true starting point", sees in "The Salvation of Swithin Forsyte" a reflection of what happened to Galsworthy and Ada during their years of hidden love affair; Swithin is the most English of men who becomes infatuated with unpossessable beauty and therefore throughout his life misses the intensity of real emotion. Galsworthy himself, of course, was bolder, possessed himself of the dream and in consequence was able to live fully, to transform himself from an idle young Forsyte into the artist he became. But this is probably to make too much of a single story, although there were undoubtedly elements of Galsworthy's own situation woven into it; he described all his writing at this time as "an endless duel fought out within a man between the emotional and critical sides of his nature". But that the story had no particular significance for Galsworthy himself is evident from his treatment of it. When he came to republish it seven years later, bound up with the three other stories and with *Villa Rubein*, he subjected it to so drastic a revision that he cut its length by one-fifth, taking much of his cue from criticisms that Hueffer had expressed on its first writing.

Nevertheless, there is substance in Mottram's view that A *Man of Devon* was the true starting-point. For the first time, Galsworthy was writing in consistently adult style—with some bad lapses into over-writing and melodrama still occurring as, for example, in the bathetic ending of "The Salvation of Swithin". It marks out the Forsytes as his writing territory; there is, indeed, the first mention of old Jolyon, presiding wisely over the affairs of his mining company, aloof and steadfast in a neurotic boardroom. Also, this was the first volume to suggest to the small literary circle around Conrad that the latter's protégé might have in him the stuff of a considerable writer. Hueffer wrote sensibly about "Swithin Forsyte" as "far and away the best thing you have done".

Edward Garnett was sufficiently taken with it to turn aside to instruct Galsworthy as he had never troubled to before. Conrad himself, abandoning the excessive flattery, sent him a deeply-thought letter of advice: "The fact is you want more scepticism at the very foundation of your work. Scepticism, the tonic of minds, the tonic of life, the agent of truth—the way of art and salvation. In a book you should love the idea and be scrupulously faithful to your conception of life. There lies the honour of the writer, not in the fidelity of his personages. You must never allow them to decoy you out of yourself. As against your people you must preserve an attitude of perfect indifference—the part of creative power.... Your attitude to them should be purely intellectual, more independent, freer, less rigorous than it is. You seem for their sake to hug your conceptions of right and wrong too closely. There is exquisite atmosphere in your tales. What they want now is more air."

A *Man of Devon* was published in the autumn of 1901, and shortly afterwards there came a momentous change in Galsworthy's private and secret life. There was news that Major Arthur was about to return from the Boer War. The interval during which Ada had been freed from whatever tortures her married life caused her was soon to end. At this point, she and young John decided that it would be impossible to return to the life they had earlier led. Before her husband arrived back in England, Ada moved out of his house in South Kensington and took a flat for herself in Campden House Chambers on Campden Hill, just round the corner from her lover and close to the homes of his sisters and his parents. She did not as yet openly live with Galsworthy, but her removal from Major Arthur's house made explicit to the whole family (except still, it seems, to old John) the situation which until then had been certainly known, but resolutely ignored. Now, however, Major Arthur's mother wrote to tell him not to return to South Kensington, but to rejoin his parental home in Queen's Gate when he got back from South Africa. In this letter she broke to him the news that his wife had left him and that she was carrying on an affair with his cousin. Major Arthur told his second wife that this was the first notion he had had that Ada was unfaithful to him.

In spite of his previous indifference to her, he was desperately angry and unhappy. It is clear from the few comments that in later years he made to Mrs Wilhelmine that he felt the insult keenly. Ever since his school days, she said, he had laboured under a sense of being something of a failure and he saw Ada's defection as yet another instance of his own inadequacy.

The question that arises is why Major Arthur, arriving home in England angry and unhappy, did not at once start proceedings for divorce. For nearly three more years he did nothing, took no steps but continued to live at Queen's Gate in idle misery. Mrs Wilhelmine believed that he wanted to get a divorce immediately but was restrained by his own parents. They were not acting in any broad spirit of tolerance, for they were as angry at the whole thing as was their son. In Marrot's account, derived from Ada, it is declared that "the attitude of the family as a whole was unfailingly friendly (to the young lovers); even—and this is noteworthy—that of the immediate family of her first husband". There seems to be no evidence to confirm this. According to Mrs Wilhelmine, it was simply not true, and the affair split the Galsworthy family in two. The reason, she said, that Frederick Galsworthy, the estate agent and auctioneer, forbade his son to seek a divorce was only to avoid a public scandal. He acted just in the manner that Galsworthy was to make Soames's father, James, act when, in *The Man of Property*, he realizes that his son's wife has a lover. A possible scandal—do almost anything to avoid that. So long as Ada was not living openly with young

John the matter could remain reasonably private. So long as he remained in the studio above the stable in Aubrey Walk and she in the flat in Campden House Chambers and they conducted their journeys abroad with discretion, there would be no open scandal and the family would not have to suffer its formidable consequences.

The reason that Major Arthur obeyed his parents was that he had no choice. He, too, was living on an allowance from his father and it seems to have been made clear to him that, if he brought the scandal into the open by divorce proceedings, that allowance would be imperilled. So he supinely did nothing. He may well have decided that to lose an unsatisfactory wife was bad enough in its way and wounding to his esteem, but to lose also his comfort and leisure to devote to the Yeomanry would be intolerable.

X

During this time Galsworthy wrote, revised and rewrote assiduously, acquiring technique, a skill. He also defined his attitudes towards society which determined his kind of writing. They were inextricably mixed with his personal life. He himself referred to the impulse behind his writing at this time as due to "the ferment roused in my spirit by the Boer War and to a simmering revolt against the shibboleths of my home, my school and college". Undoubtedly the ten years or so of Kiplingesque jingoism which gripped the English as never before or since, culminating in the Queen's jubilee and the Boer War, aroused a repulsion in Galsworthy, as in all liberal-minded men. But he was already in his thirty-fourth year, too old to be inflamed by this alone. What started the simmering revolt against the shibboleths of his home, school and college—against, that is, the whole of late-Victorian, wealthy middle-class society—was its treatment of Ada. Even his antagonism to the Boer War may have been at least coloured by the knowledge that Major Arthur was taking part in it. The poverty which he saw around him in London, which he had been investigating with fascinated disquiet ever since those early night-wanderings of the slum streets, was a strong influence on his naturally sympathetic mind but not the chief one. Society's threatened punishment of Ada was the main motive for his attack on it, the most vivid symbol of its hypocrisy and rottenness. This was what he was trying to set down in most of the work he struggled to accomplish during the three years from 1901 to 1904 when he published nothing. He was trying to define his attitude towards life and his own times and the stages by which he had arrived at it. In doing so, he provided himself with virtually all the material he would need for the sustained literary work of the following ten years during which he established himself and provided himself too with the technique of his art.

The first attempt he made to force into the shape of written words the ferment and personal anger inside him was in the form of a play, *The Civilized*. Although he never completed it, substantial parts of it remain in manuscript and typescript. It deals with James Forsyte and his wife, recognizably the beginnings of the characters in *The Forsyte Saga*, whose son, here called George, is in a similar situation with his wife, Helen, as Soames was to be with Irene—and, to some extent, as Major Arthur had been with Ada. George and Helen, completely dependent financially on his father, are themselves estranged. Mrs James, in the play, uses precisely the same expression as Major Arthur's second wife recalled Major Arthur himself using about Ada. They were not "on terms". The conflict between George and Helen in this early attempt at a play, however, is far cruder and less sensitive than that which Galsworthy was to create between Soames and Irene in the *Saga*; or, indeed, than that which in fact seems to have existed between Ada and Major Arthur, though not perhaps than the exaggerated account which Ada herself had given of her misery. George Forsyte, in this play, is brutal and a boor, a bully and a coward. They have a child, but Mrs James has discovered that the child is not her son's. The real father, who has died, was brother to Helen's closest woman friend. When George knows the paternity of the child he thought was his, he wildly threatens a divorce, then retracts for fear of a public scandal. Helen walks out, taking her child to the refuge of her friend's house. The Forsytes plead with her to come back in order to still people's tongues. By the time the play breaks off, unfinished, it is fairly clear that in the ending which Galsworthy purposed, she would go back to her husband in beaten, wearied misery.

Here, then, he had found the courage to tackle the one theme that was vital to him, the theme of Ada's marriage. In the course of even this first and unsuccessful attempt to develop it, he found that it inevitably enmeshed him in two other themes—a satirical attack on contemporary moneyed society as a whole and at the same time a deep and inborn admiration for it. The rebellion was not a true one; far deeper in his emotions lay a respect for the very class against which he was rebelling and this he expressed by portraits of stoical, wise, compassionate old men, drawn from his love of his father. These conflicts and these themes constitute all of importance that he was to write about until the First World War swept away the strongly conventional society that had wounded Ada and allowed him to reinstate her in that place of respect and within his own class which he had always deeply desired that, as his wife, she should occupy as of right.

He abandoned *The Civilized* unfinished because he came to realize that the task was beyond him. During 1901 he showed it to Conrad, who found it "too promising to let go", but was clearly unhappy about it. He made one suggestion that could have eradicated some of the play's crudity and melodrama, that the child should have died before the action began. Galsworthy adopted the suggestion and began to try it out, but by the time he had worked it into only the opening scene, he realized that the whole play was hopeless and put it aside. He was still blinded by his personal emotions when he came to write about Ada. Impossible for him, as yet, to take any sort of detached view, because what would happen to her and to him in real life was still to be discovered when Major Arthur should return from South Africa.

When he abandoned the play and returned to the form of

the novel, in which he had at least some apprentice experience, he therefore also excluded from it any direct reference to Ada. Two things remained. The first was the world of poverty around him and his shuddering, fascinated probings of it; the second the development of his own mind, his own principles to live by, during those earlier years when, stirred by Georg Sauter's entry onto the scene at Cambridge Gate and then by his own growing love for Ada, he began to question the small society of privilege and power in which he had been brought up. If he confined the book to these two subjects, then he could use all the social satire which he had begun to work out in the unfinished play. But the satirical element in it is still clumsy and unimpressive. The value of this book, when it was at last published as *The Island Pharisees*, lies in the self-portrait of Galsworthy as a young man emerging into adult life. It was also the book in which he began to take lessons from Edward Garnett, who had evidently by this time come to the opinion that he was worth taking in hand. Here he was created as the writer the world was to know; Ada herself, with her customary shrewdness of judgment, declared even before it was published that this was perhaps the first book in which Jack, at "thirty-six or so", was really himself. It was also the first which he signed with his own name.

Galsworthy has documented the origin and development of this novel. On one of his journeys to Paris he met by chance a young Belgian tramp named Clermont, a wandering ne'er-do-well with a bitter gift of expression, who later died of tuberculosis. From time to time they afterwards wrote to each other and Galsworthy gave Clermont money—he was ever open-handed with money. He wrote that Clermont disclosed to him "the world of failures, of the rolling stones, the underworld". But this was not quite accurate. For years he had been wandering in just such a world in London. What seems more likely is that the articulate bitterness of this particular young tramp summed up for Galsworthy in one person all the sympathy he felt for those who suffered poverty; and this was sufficient to set him at work in August 1901 on a long picaresque novel, at first called *The Pagan*. In this, not only was the central character a portrait of Clermont—lightly disguised as Louis Ferrand, the other half of the place-name which his true name suggested—but the book was written from the point of view of the tramp himself, and told in the first person.

When it was nearly finished, Galsworthy had an attack of those sudden doubts of the value of the whole thing from which he was long to suffer. So he sent the manuscript to Edward Garnett for his opinion. Garnett soon confirmed the doubts. It was hopeless for Galsworthy to try to put himself into a person so foreign in every way to his own nature. "No, my dear fellow," said Garnett, as Galsworthy reported the conversation, "It's all very well, but you shouldn't have done that fellow subjectively. You can't possibly know the real inside of a vagabond like that; you ought to give him to us objectively, through a personality like your own."

Galsworthy obediently set himself to the task of rewriting the book. Or, rather, he wrote a completely fresh book, retaining only one or two of the characters of *The Pagan*, three of its episodes and not a single one of its sentences. He says that he then "conceived Shelton" as a new central character through whose eyes the story could be seen. In fact, what he did was to put his own younger self into the book—the young man down from Oxford, called to the Bar but abandoning the career of law—and call him Shelton. He then tried to contrast the two points of view, that of himself as Shelton, representing the black-coated society, and Ferrand the penniless vagrant. Rewriting the book took Galsworthy a further year, so that it was already 1902 by the time he showed the new version to Garnett, who once more shook his head. "Do it again," he said. Galsworthy himself knew that the book was still wrong—he later admitted that he had made a "half-baked job" of it. He therefore undertook a third complete re-writing, in which the whole of the narrative is seen through the eyes of Shelton who, stirred by Ferrand's bitter comments from the depths of poverty, is brought to question and reject the set of conventional values in which he had been brought up. The attitude of the world he faces is summed up by his uncle, Paramor, a solicitor: "Isn't life bad enough already? ... Truth's the very devil. ... Feelings are snakes! only fit to be kept in bottles with tight corks." The attitude towards the terrifying poverty in the back streets of London is either that of the warden of a charitable club for working men who refuses money to a destitute young couple with three children because they are not married ("We make a point of not encouraging sin, of course."), or that of the wealthy woman whose hobby is slumming ("Oh, do tell us about the slums, Mrs Mattock! Slumming must be splendid!" "The poor are not the least bit what you think of them ... they do nothing but grumble."). A scene in which Shelton returns to Oxford to revisit his former tutor gives Galsworthy the chance of a backward glance at what Oxford meant to him. The conversation between the dons is stilted, highly conventional and stupid: one of them, picking up a copy of *Madame Bovary*, comments, "Imagine a man writing that stuff if ever he'd been at Eton! What do we want to know about that sort of thing? A writer should be a sportsman and a gentleman." Shelton muses, "I was a snob when I was up here. I believed all I was told, anything that made life pleasant." As always, too, Galsworthy could not resist an irrelevant reference to Ada's situation. He introduced a young man, living in the country with a woman who is not his wife and who is conse-

94

quently cut by the county. Even when she is hurt in a slight riding accident, Shelton is prevented from helping her by the strait-laced young beauty to whom he is engaged. His cry at everything is, "We all want our money's worth, our pound of flesh! Pity we use such fine words—'Society. Religion. Morality.' Humbug!"

The triple writing of *The Island Pharisees* did not make it into a good novel. Some years later, when it was to be republished—with a dedication to Garnett's wife—Galsworthy revised it extensively yet again and in the process cut a thousand words out of it. But it still limped. Getting it published in the first place proved difficult. Several publishers rejected it, and it was only when Conrad intervened to recommend it to Heinemann—a recommendation that over the years must have proved among the most valuable that house ever got— that in 1904 the first novel signed by Galsworthy's own name was published. It was not well received by most critics, who made the just comment that it was not really a novel at all but a string of anecdotes trying to make propaganda points. It was not widely sold. Among those of his own class who read it, it gained for Galsworthy the reputation of being a "bit of a socialist". But it had no ponderable influence in general.

The importance of the book, of course, was to the author himself. It may have cleared in his mind his attitude towards the society in which he lived; it certainly enabled Garnett to teach him his craft. During the third writing, he was sent the manuscript as it was written, piece by piece, almost chapter by chapter; he and Galsworthy met frequently to discuss it. Conrad, from the side, put forward more suggestions, more criticisms. It was perhaps scarcely to be expected that, in such circumstances, the thrice-written book could retain much freshness of originality. But the lessons were nonetheless valuable. For Galsworthy carried out the third writing of *The*

Island Pharisees during 1903, alternating it with work on a new novel he had started in May of that year, which at first he thought of calling *The Forsyte Saga*, but which was to appear under the title of *The Man of Property*.

XI

During those years of literary struggle and hesitation Galsworthy suffering such periods of frustration that he almost abandoned altogether his ambition to write. In 1904 he produced a comic short story, "The Consummation", in which he summed up with a wry grin his writing career as he saw it at that point; *The Island Pharisees* had just appeared. The short story concerns a young man (as it might be Galsworthy), who is urged by a young lady on a railway station to adopt writing as a career and consequently produces a book of short stories and pays for its publication. It sells four hundred copies and is flatteringly reviewed. He happens to know a man of genius (as it might be Conrad) who encourages him to write a longer story which is refused by his first publisher but accepted by a younger on terms of a postponed royalty. It is less well reviewed and sells only three hundred copies. While writing his third book, the author is introduced by the man of genius to a well known critic (as it might be Garnett), who is equally encouraging; when the third book is published, it sells two hundred copies. The fourth book is highly praised by the man of genius, although, in fact, he finds himself unable to read more than six chapters of it. The fifth book is extravagantly praised by the critic, who, after reading a few pages, makes his wife read the rest; the fifth book has only one review, and absolutely no sale. When the author has finished his sixth book, he takes it out to a secluded spot on Hampstead Heath to read it quietly through. But after three chapters, he sits with his head buried in his hands: "He had indeed exhausted his public. It was *too* good—he could not read it himself!"

Conrad was immensely tickled when Galsworthy sent him this short story. So, no doubt, was Garnett. Galsworthy himself, plodding doggedly on with the two novels on which he was engaged, wondered grimly now and again whether he, too, should not quietly place his manuscripts in a drawer, and never write another word. He was having such a struggle with *The Man of Property*, of which in a year he had completed the draft of not much more than a third, and that with all the tortures of false starts, revisions and rewriting—Garnett nursed him through that phase. In June of 1904 they went on a walking tour together, pupil and master, and Galsworthy returned from it with a refreshed hope that something could be made of this theme which he had already once abandoned in the uncompleted play. Later that summer he and Ada went again to their beloved Italian Alps. In the autumn they returned to London, she to her flat on Campden Hill, and he to his mews studio in Aubrey Walk, to grapple resolutely with the novel, of which, with continuing difficulty, he finished drafting some two-thirds by the end of the year.

In December his father died. When, in the preceding year, old John's wife had left him and taken a flat, alone, in Kensington Palace Mansions, he had given up his own establishment and gone to live for a time with Tom and Mabel Reynolds in Tor Gardens, and then with Lilian and Georg Sauter at 1 Holland Park Avenue. There at least he had the solace of his grandson Rudo, who can remember him even then, despite his eighty-six years, as a vigorous old man who would still put on his tall silk hat and make his daily journey to the City, on fine days walking across the Park. But the autumn of the following year proved too much for him. Throughout October and November he lay in an upstairs room of his daughter's house, constantly attended by his son John, who sat hour by hour at his bedside reading Dickens to him. At the beginning of December, at eighty-seven years of age, old

John died, and at once his son's life was radically changed.

The old man left an estate proved at £110,305 18s. 6d. gross, disposing of it in a will composed in the grand Victorian manner; including four long codicils, it runs magnificently through thirteen pages of the records at Somerset House. As executors and trustees he appointed his son John, Tom Reynolds and a nephew, E. H. Galsworthy, a solicitor with whom old John was in partnership. He later added Georg Sauter to the list and removed the solicitor.

By his main will, made in 1896, he left his wife Blanche an outright sum of £500, an annuity of £800 a year, and the right to take £500's worth of furniture from the house to set her up in a smaller residence. To each of his children he left an outright payment of £100 and £400 a year. The rest of his estate was to be divided into equal shares for his children five years after his death (this was later increased to seven years). The sons were to have their shares absolutely, and the daughters' shares were to be held in trust for them and their children.

In 1903, the year in which Blanche left him, he added a long codicil which reduced her outright legacy to £200 and revoked her permission to take any of the furniture, since she had already chosen what she wanted. Her annuity was unchanged.

The codicil also raised young John's immediate legacy from £100 to £2,500, free of duty; materially improved Mabel's position; granted Georg and Lilian a long lease at a low rent on the house at Holland Park Avenue; and settled more than £5,000 in trust for the favourite grandchild, Rudo Sauter, to go to him absolutely at the age of twenty-one. Moreover, all four children's incomes were raised from £400 to £700 a year. A later codicil, added shortly before old John's death, settled £3,500 on two more grandchildren, Muriel Galsworthy (Hubert's daughter) and Owen Reynolds (Mabel's son).

Immediately upon his father's death, therefore, Galsworthy gained financial independence with a prompt legacy of £2,500, an income of £700 a year and a large inheritance to come seven years later.

But his father's death made one other change in his life even more radical than that. Whether the motive for concealing his relationship with Ada from his father had been a determination not to wound him, or a fear lest the old man might cut off his income—or, perhaps, a mixture of both—the obstacle was now removed. He and Ada could create the open scandal which would compel the family to allow Major Arthur to seek a divorce. They therefore went away together to a farmhouse on the edge of Dartmoor.

It was called Wingstone farm, just outside the village of Manaton which lies between Bovey Tracey and Moretonhampstead. Some years later the Galsworthys were to establish their country home in this house and for years it was his retreat from life; she never really liked it, since the dampness of the place affected her rheumatism. He had come across it in the first place one Sunday evening on a June walking tour, being directed to it from the village inn, which was full; the farmer let out part of his house to guests in the summer. The place had at once attracted him. The moment he got into the field of buttercups before the house, he felt within himself "a peculiar contentment, and sat down on a rock to let the feeling grow . . . all hill and hollow, long ago reclaimed from the moor; and against the distant folds of the hills the farmhouse and its thatched barns were just visible, embowered amongst beeches and some dark trees, with a soft bright crown of sunlight over the whole. . . . Leaving the rock at last, I went towards the house. It was long and low and rather sad, standing in a garden all mossy grass and buttercups, with a few rhododendrons and flowery shrubs below a fine row of old Irish yews."

According to Marrot, this walking tour took place in 1904, and must therefore have been that which Galsworthy shared with Garnett, as they earnestly discussed the problems of his novel. But either Marrot made a slip, or Ada, even after her husband's death, was trying to cover up their life together before they married. The implication is that Galsworthy found Wingstone by chance in the summer of 1904, and took her there in December, after the death of his father, to get her divorce in train. But in the private note she left of their travels together she records that they had been at Wingstone twice before, at Easter 1903 and Easter 1904. Those earlier visits were, of course, discreet and unnoticed. But the December 1904 visit was deliberately announced to provide Major Arthur with grounds for his divorce proceedings. He took the opportunity proffered to him and served them with papers of divorce petition. The case was set down for March 1905. They had, of course, no intention of defending it. Galsworthy had already made exact preparations, resigned from his club and his boards and set about buying a house in Addison Road, Kensington. He had no intention, either, of submitting Ada to the ordeal of London and her friends while the divorce was going through. Directly the papers had been served he took her abroad. They left London on January 10, making as always for Italy. In his bag was the unfinished manuscript of *The Man of Property*, the theme of which had now been overtaken by events.

XII

They went first to Levanto, where they settled into the Grand Hotel and Galsworthy resumed work on his novel. Now that he and Ada were openly together, he found it immensely easier to write. "It was written here, there and everywhere," he recorded at the end of his life, "the most scattered of my manuscripts at the time of my life most poignant. Two-thirds of it had taken nearly two years to write; the last third was written in six weeks, with the pale north Italian sunlight filtering through the winter branches on to the pages. . . . When, seven years later, we were changing house, I came upon fragments of the first two-thirds of *The Man of Property*. Instantly I lighted a fire and stuffed them into it, an incredible confusion of jumbled notebook pages. The last third, clean-written with the continuity of a mind at rest, I had not the heart to preserve. Into the fire it went too."

By February 1 Galsworthy was reporting to Garnett that he had only two and a half chapters to write in order to finish the book: "After that, a month for revision and Ada to type the whole through, and then I shall send it to England." He had by now thought of the title, *The Man of Property*, about which he asked Garnett's opinion. Indeed, he badly wanted him to read the whole manuscript once more—invited him to come out to Italy to do so, at Galsworthy's expense—before he handed it over to Sydney Pawling of Heinemann. He did not want to come out before he and Ada were married, which meant not earlier than October.

Before he quite finished the writing, he and Ada had moved on to Rome, Naples and then Amalfi. Conrad and his wife Jessie were taking a holiday on Capri. Galsworthy and Ada crossed over to visit them, and found Conrad quite unable to work—the mishaps and the crushing expense of the holiday had proved quite too much for his spirit—but enthusiastically recommending Norman Douglas, then a young man just starting to write. While the Galsworthys were there, a false alarm of fire in their hotel at night brought them rushing from their room, hastily throwing a few valuables into a bag; only later did they realize that they had not packed the manuscript of *The Man of Property*, the only copy then in existence.

By the time they left Sorrento to journey northwards, stopping once more at Rome, then Florence, then Bologna, the first draft of the novel was complete and Ada had typed two copies. Galsworthy vastly emended one and sent the other home to Lilian for safety, in some boxes of possessions he was despatching. He was quite exhausted, partly from the sustained effort of finishing the novel, partly from a slight sunstroke. From an hotel on the Austrian side of the Mendel Pass he wrote to Garnett that, directly he heard that the boxes had arrived safely in Kensington, he would send him the first fully revised manuscript. The letter to Garnett was one of warm gratitude for all his tuition, all his care: "You are the one of us who cannot be spared; the Conrads, the Hudsons, the Hueffers, the Bellocs, and above all myself can be spared, but for some reason or another which perhaps I couldn't put into words but which I feel intensely, *you* cannot be spared. So much for the public side. On the private side, still less."

Lilian duly wired to announce the safe arrival of the boxes, so on May 16 Galsworthy sent the top copy of the manuscript to Garnett, who had undertaken to hand it to Pawling. Galsworthy had thought of asking £50 in advance of a royalty of 15 per cent, rising to 20 per cent after the sale of 2,000 copies. The Forsytean qualities in him were evident in the proposal.

He registered and insured the parcel containing the manuscript, explaining that it was the only complete copy, that he was nervous about it and could scarcely face the task of revising the second copy should the first be lost. He asked that Garnett should have it retyped—"*well* typed with specially careful *supervision* for which I will pay special rates, also for expedition". Then the fresh copy was to be handed to Pawling and the original sent round to 1 Holland Park Avenue for Lilian to read—she must evidently have been instructed not to look at the manuscript sent to her in the boxes, for it was only a draft.

Finally, of course, Galsworthy wanted Garnett and his wife to read it. He would be most anxious to have their opinions of it. He would be "nervous till I receive your impressions".

He was in fact now in a state of such desperate anxiety as to the merit or demerit of this novel, which he already knew to be the best he could do, that he found himself wishing that he had never attempted a literary career. "Sometimes there comes over one now the feeling," he wrote from Austria to Garnett, "that in pure physical health and pleasures lies the true existence, and that in all the nerve devouring and heart searching and analysis of our·present years lies discontent and fag. How comparatively and vegetably happy are not one or two of my friends of those [Oxford] days who have been content to pass their lives keeping packs of hounds. No doubts and queries about them! Jolly red faces, and solid muscles. Ah! well, everything that is, is right. I'm going to take up riding again seriously when I come back, and make Ada too. She used to be terribly fond of it before life knocked her about. And I have dreams of you on a Dartmoor nag next summer with us. You must come to us—all of you, and wander over the moor—there are such jolly farms to be got, and we mean to get one for the best weather next year."

This was, however, merely nervous posturing while he waited for Garnett to say what he thought of the third part of the novel; he had already read the first two parts, in which the story of the Forsyte family, in their prosperous houses set around Hyde Park, is carried forward to the point at which Soames Forsyte's wife, Irene, having long found her marriage to be a failure and a torment to her, and having now fallen in love with Bosinney, the penniless young architect who is building Soames's house at Coombe, breaks off her relationship with her husband by locking him from her bedroom. In spite of Bosinney's engagement to June Forsyte, Irene's cousin and dearest friend, and although a scandal would ruin his life, their passion drives them secretly together; but Soames, seeing Irene return to his house one afternoon, flushed with happiness when she thought she was unobserved, knows exactly what she means when, to his fierce question, "And where may you have been?" she defiantly replies, "In heaven—out of this house!"

All these first two parts, written so laboriously over a period of two years, Garnett had already approved. He had recognized—with some touch of astonishment, of reluctance and even of jealousy—the manner in which the characters of the Forsytes had been built up with the touches of greatness peculiar to the English comic novel. From the very first and splendid paragraph, Galsworthy had pulled it off—this most difficult feat of all English prose writing, "Those privileged to be present at a family festival of the Forsytes have seen that charming and instructive sight—an upper middle-class family in full plumage. But whosoever of these favoured persons has possessed the gift of psychological analysis (a talent without monetary value and properly ignored by the Forsytes), has witnessed a spectacle, not only delightful in itself, but illustrative of an obscure human problem. In plainer words, he has gleaned from a gathering of this family—no branch of which had a liking for the other, between no three members of whom existed anything worthy of the name of sympathy—evidence of that mysterious concrete tenacity which renders a family so formidable a unit of society, so clear a reproduction of society in miniature. He has been admitted to a vision of the dim roads of social progress, has understood something of patriarchal life, or the swarmings of savage hordes, or the rise and fall of nations."

They were there already, the essentially English family (which so many hundreds of people were to claim as so similar to their own that Galsworthy must surely have had some knowledge of them). He picked them out one by one. Aunt Ann, the senior, sitting with inflexible back, knitting or reading in a corner of her brother Timothy's green drawing-room under the ægis of a plume of dyed pampas grass in a light blue vase. Swithin, the stout bachelor wearing two waistcoats and a ruby pin, and his lean, anxious twin James, his grey eyes with an air of fixed absorption in some secret worry, nervously turning in his hands a piece of china and declaring that it wasn't real old Worcester. Old Jolyon, the head of the family, the patriarch who for all his gentleness must not be thwarted. Soames Forsyte, the man of property himself, the cautious solicitor, flat-shouldered, clean-shaven, flat-cheeked, flat-waisted, looking downwards and aslant as though trying to see through the side of his own nose; Soames, an honourable man, having no particular bad qualities except a certain meanness and the undefinable quality of simply being unlovable.

The skill and the virtue of all this Garnett had already perceived, and the magnificent catch of the whole of that segment of Victorian society and manners, a re-creation of their London, their England, their world, in the sense that, for example, Thackeray had re-created the world of *Vanity Fair*. Galsworthy was later to claim that in these pages he had pickled the upper middle-class, placed it "under glass for strollers in the wide and ill-arranged museum of Letters to gaze at. Here it rests, preserved in its own juice; the Sense of

Property." The claim was just. When he read the first two parts of the novel, Garnett must have stared. Here was the man who, so far as the technique of his craft was concerned, was virtually his pupil, and it began to look as though he might pull off something extraordinary. While he could not have been expected at that stage to comprehend the whole achievement, there is evidence in his letters that already he had the feeling that here could be something imperishable.

Then, in the registered, insured package from the Austrian Alps, came the third part, which Galsworthy had written with such ease and lightness in the pale Italian winter sunshine, now that Ada had been rescued from the situation in which he had left his fictional Irene. When he read it, Garnett let out a growl of dismay. He approved of the development of the story as Galsworthy had at first continued it. On a certain foggy night of late November, Irene has inadvertently left her bedroom door unlocked and Soames, who has been inflamed into an acute jealousy by gossip thrown at him, steals upon her asleep and "exerts his rights and acts like a man". (Garnett did not even object, as he well might have done, to the clumsy explanations which Galsworthy thought necessary of what had really occurred; such as having Soames read in *The Times*, on his way to the City next morning, of the unusually high number of cases of rape to come before the grand jury— as though the author could not expect the reader to take the thing obliquely, but nervously underlined it, so that it should not be missed.) Soames commits this act of property a couple of days before his case against Bosinney is to come to court. He is suing him for having exceeded the financial limits given him in building the house at Coombe and knows that the case will ruin him and thus revenge Soames on his wife's lover. All this Garnett took to be well. "For the imagination, and insight, and working out of most of the pages I have the strongest admiration," he wrote to Galsworthy. "There are

107

many passages which beat all you have written before. . . .
The whole thing lives and breathes, it grows stronger and
stronger and more absorbing up to June's visit—and then
you seem to me to take the wrong road and stick to
it."

The "June's visit" to which he refers is the visit by the
jilted June to Bosinney's rooms, determined to make her last
effort to win him back to her. In the empty rooms she meets
Irene who, having left Soames, is also searching for Bosinney.
Soames has won his case against the architect in his absence,
for he has not appeared in court. In the first draft of the novel,
which Galsworthy had sent back for Garnett's comment, the
reason for Bosinney's absence was that, Irene having told him
of her husband's assault upon her, and he having also been
ruined in his career by the law case, he commits suicide. Then
there is nothing for Irene to do but to go dazedly back to
Soames's house, to her husband, to the marriage which is by
now filled with unutterable suffering but which she cannot
escape.

It was the suicide which brought the protest from Garnett.
"An artistic blot," he wrote to Galsworthy, "of a very grave
order, psychologically false, and seriously shaking the illusion
of the whole story." It was out of keeping with all that had
previously been learned about Bosinney. The financial ruin
involved in the law case would not have meant nearly so
much to a man of his type as Galsworthy had supposed—"to
make him commit suicide through money is to make money
paramount. But it isn't." He urged Galsworthy, as friend and
critic, most strongly to reconsider the suicide. Mrs Garnett,
he added, agreed. They felt that either Bosinney should meet
his death accidentally in the fog, or "make Bosinney and Irene
go off, personifying Youth and Joy, the indestructibility of
Love, with £50 and *her* Jewels! say £30 worth!—go bang out
into the world, leaving Soames and the jewel case, and all the

Forsyte gang with their blasted hereditaments powerless behind them".

The letter went on and on, suggesting many small improvements but insisting on none except for the one point—"don't make Bosinney commit suicide. That is my instinctive and most deliberate judgment."

By the time he received this letter Galsworthy and Ada had moved on, high into the mountains on the Italian side at Madonna di Campiglio. It was a severe blow to him. The numbness of having written was beginning to wear off and he was coming to feel ever more hopeful that he had accomplished a good piece of work. Then came this letter from his mentor, the man above all in whose judgment he trusted, striking at the very climax of his conception of the novel; striking, moreover (as Garnett must have known, but in the fervour of literary criticism had perhaps forgotten) at the truth that Galsworthy felt he had distilled from his own desperate, wretched years when Ada was still the wife of his cousin.

He found the letter waiting for him at the Hotel des Alpes and at once sat down to reply to it, though he had only just completed a nine-hour drive to reach the place. He had to answer at once, "because this looks like being the first real split in art between us (for God's sake don't let's have it in anything else)".

What made him despair was that Garnett had completely failed to see the real reason for Bossiney's suicide; not financial ruin—of course not—but because of the torment of learning from Irene that Soames had outraged her: "I feel humiliated and justly humiliated that I've not made it clear. The fact is that I wrote a chapter between Irene and Bosinney travelling in the Underground with that for motif." The last traces of that scene still remain in the final text. "I subsequently took it out because I wanted to give Bosinney indirectly, feeling as I still feel that this is the only way for *me* to do him—in other words I haven't enough power over him or insight enough into him. And doing it the second way I've obviously overdone it."

But all this he could arrange in revision. What appalled him was that Garnett and his wife wanted him to end the book with " 'a palpable and obvious defeat of Forsyteism by making the lovers run away happily'. To my mind (and I desire to defeat Forsyteism) the only way to do so is to leave the Forsytes masters of the field. The only way to enlist the sympathies of readers on the other side, the only way to cap the purpose of the book, which was to leave property as *an empty shell*—is to leave the victory to Soames. . . . This is tragic."

On a purely literary level Galsworthy's despair was justified. Garnett, with an obtuseness rare in him, had missed the point; he was himself tired, overworked, frustrated. Even in the first version of the novel it was clear that the reason for Bosinney's suicide was the outrage on the woman with whom he was in love—"perhaps the greatest mental shock a man terribly in love can have," Galsworthy pleaded. Certainly, too, a happy ending for Bosinney and Irene, running off together to Paris, personifying Youth and Joy and the indestructibility of Love, would have cheapened, falsified, and indeed nullified the novel. On the deeper personal level the wound was more painful still. If Garnett was right, then the things that he had to say in justification of himself and Ada were spurious. Ada became simply a discontented wife, wearying of her husband and running away with her lover, and his own conduct unscrupulous and sordid rather than high-minded and idealistic. That was the deep stab in Garnett's letter. Only if he could have adopted Garnett's "happy ending", would he so have tarnished his own conception of the ideals of love shared between Ada and himself that his own suicide—once considered, perhaps, and rejected—might have become even remotely possible.

Before he went to bed that night in the Hotel des Alpes, he sadly concluded his reply: "Your letter is so good, and true, and touching to me, that I am cast down to the ground." This was simply the pupil acknowledging the reproof of his teacher, for Garnett's letter was in fact neither good nor true. "Do you think," Galsworthy added in a postscript searching for one touch of comfort, "it was dangerous perhaps to read the book in parts, forming so to speak your own story for the end, before it came to you?"

With that he went to bed, but not to sleep. All night he lay there, turning over desperately in his mind what Garnett had said. By morning he was writing again, and was beginning to weaken. It was both a strength and a weakness of Galsworthy's mind and of his essential good nature, that he could always defer to a view opposed to his own. The amount of advice and interference he accepted in completing his major novel is, indeed, astonishing. By his side stood Ada, discussing with him every word, every incident, every motive of character; and, necessarily, discussing it from the point of view of the woman who knew she was the model for Irene, and whose own life was, obliquely, being argued. She, too, was against the suicide, for the feminine and obviously personal reason that she did not believe a man would desert a woman in such trouble. Then from London came a series of letters from Garnett and his wife, urging with a remarkable lack of humility large alterations in a novel which they could see to be important, and which was not theirs. All this Galsworthy accepted and a considerable part of it acceded to. It was almost authorship by committee.

In the letter he wrote from the hotel, after his sleepless night, he was standing out strongly against any happy ending. He wrote to Garnett, "My dear fellow, if I do so much as wink the eye in favour of the lovers, if I so much as hint at their victory and happiness the book is destroyed." But already he was weakening about Bosinney's suicide. Perhaps, he admitted, he had made a mistake in *time* over this. In the first draft, Bosinney had committed suicide on the afternoon of the court case, when he had learned of his financial ruin. Galsworthy now conceded that "the suicide would most probably have come about under the wheels of a bus in the fog, instead of the following afternoon. I can alter this, with but little change; and if you like I can leave it in the mind of the reader as it would be in the minds of the Jury, doubtful whether it was suicide or no. I will contrive a way of making it more patent that when George [Forsyte] is following him in the fog, he is straight from the Confession" (by Irene, of what Soames has done).

By the evening, having posted the morning's letter, he was writing to Garnett again. Perhaps, after all, he could put in Bosinney's death as accident *or* suicide, leaving it vague. He was so rattled by all this that he moved on from his hotel into another in the Dolomites, at San Martino di Castrozza. All the time, as he hints in his letters to Garnett, he carried on an equally intense discussion with Ada as to whether Bosinney should be seen as committing suicide or whether his death should be accidental. Scarcely had he settled into his new hotel when there came a fresh letter from Garnett. Very well, make him killed in the fog but don't even imply suicide. Garnett dismissed the fact that, on his first reading, he had quite missed the point: "I regard suicide through the shock of the rape to be as incredible as suicide through financial worry." He gave way on the ending; on that he told Galsworthy, "you must follow your instinct entirely. . . . The ending is very good, so long as B. *doesn't commit suicide.*"

It was more than Galsworthy could withstand. He set to work on a revision of the third part of the novel, still wandering restlessly from mountain hotel to mountain hotel. At last he began to perceive, or at least persuaded himself, that Garnett had been right. To Mrs Garnett he wrote, "I have thrown up the sponge. Between you, you have made me believe that Bosinney is really alive, and not merely a figure—haunting the book for the purposes of the story. . . . If I have really succeeded with him at all I must be in the position of the sportsman (who after missing all day brought down a bird) to whom his gamekeeper said with resignation, 'Eh! But they will fly into it sometimes!' Bosinney must have flown into it. I am conscious of feeling mentally with him early in the book, and then exerting all my artifice to keep people from seeing that I had done so; what a light this throws upon the whole of literary work! . . . I feel in a terrible muddle, and don't know how my revision will work out. I don't feel any inspiration, and I fear it will be a lame and patchwork job. Still it should be better than what is."

To Garnett, however, he was writing more cheerfully, putting up to him the odd suggestion that, after *The Man of Property* on the title page, there should be a subtitle, *National Ethics I*, or *Christian Ethics I*, or *Tales of a Christian People I*. This would enable him to write two more books to a series, carrying young Jolyon as commentator through them all—young Jolyon speaking, of course, for his author; and the whole series to be devoted to showing the feeling of utter disharmony of the Christian religion with the English character. Garnett, no doubt charitably attributing the subtitles to the effect of prolonged mountain air, was politely discouraging, and Galsworthy acquiesced; the interest lies in that he was even then regarding *The Man of Property* as the foundation stone of a series of novels, although of a very different kind from that which he ultimately built upon it.

By mid-June, Galsworthy had become so far reconciled to Garnett's views on Bosinney's suicide that he was convincing himself that the death would even "gain in strength and credibility as an accident by judicious use of a suspicion of suicide, which the reader by interior knowledge is enabled to reject". By the end of the month he was convinced that Garnett had been right all along, and even conceded some slight alteration of the ending (which, subsequently, he withdrew). By the middle of July the work was finished, the manuscript had been despatched to England, and Pawling had accepted it on Galsworthy's terms.

It was no less than just that it should be dedicated to Edward Garnett, who had in some sense formed the author and interfered so firmly, and in some ways wrongly, in the completion of the novel. For Garnett was Galsworthy's true tutor. Conrad had certainly encouraged and flattered him in his earliest days but had never succeeded in teaching him much; indeed, had never much tried to do so. Conrad was not even shown *The Man of Property* until early in 1906, when all the arguments were over and publication lay only a short time ahead. It is perhaps for this reason that his response was briefer and a shade less cordial than usual, though he was incapable of anything but politeness: "In part marvellously done and in its whole a piece of art—indubitably a piece of art. I've read it three times. My respect for you increased with every reading. I have meditated over these pages not a little. . . . By Jove, it's admirable in at least three aspects. But, I say, the Socialists ought to present you with a piece of plate."

There had already been one more argument before the book was published. When the revision was complete, a copy of the manuscript was sent round to Lilian Sauter. She was startled that her brother should have taken his own situation with Irene as the theme of his novel; it distressed her that, for all pretence of fictional divergence, some at least of the portraits of the Forsytes were recognizably those of members of the family. In particular, she objected to the portrait of their father as old Jolyon, as a lonely and pathetic old man; for this, she must have felt, was far nearer the truth between old John and Blanche than had ever before been revealed. She wrote to her brother, urging him in effect either not to publish, or to defer publication for many years, or to publish anonymously.

Galsworthy was back in England when he sat down, in the Buckingham Palace Hotel, to answer Lilian's letter. He and Ada had returned because the period of Major Arthur's decree nisi was nearly fulfilled and they would be free to marry on September 23, the day on which, in fact, they did marry. It was just under a fortnight earlier that he set himself to meet Lilian's objections to *The Man of Property*. The book, he claimed, was undoubtedly his best so far. A writer had to look near home for material to work with, and although he was not as good a writer as he wanted to be, he did not feel he was bad enough for it to be desirable for him to stop writing. He could not publish anonymously, for the book was to be the first of a series. To defer publication would be to publish never. Did she and Mabel feel strongly enough about the book to consign it to the flames? (Not, of course, that Galsworthy ever intended any such fate for it.) In any case, he asked her, what harm could be done? Who, "apart from yourself, Mab and Mother (who perhaps had better not read the book)", would know enough to link Ada with Irene, especially as he had given Irene golden hair instead of dark?

He then took up the question of which of the Forsyte characters were portraits of the Galsworthys. Swithin, Aunt Ann and old Jolyon were certainly such, so far as fictional characters could be. Aunt Juley, the silly, fussy Forsyte aunt who is continually saying the tactless thing, he admitted to be based on Blanche Galsworthy, their mother. (He did not add that June was modelled on their sister Mabel, though as yet it was only a recollection of Georg Sauter choosing between the two sisters that was obliquely reflected in the character; in later Forsyte novels, in which June develops her staunchness, her courage, her propensity for helping lame ducks, the source in Mabel would become much more apparent.)

What did any of this matter? he asked Lilian. Only the Galsworthys themselves, and a few of their intimate friends, would know enough to recognize themselves as the Forsytes. And, in the recent circumstances, which of them would be likely to read the book?

That question disposes of the suggestion (in, for example, the *Life and Letters*) that the family were sympathetic to the love between young John and Ada. The ostracism was such, outside Galsworthy's immediate family of sisters and brother, that they were not even likely to read his novel and thus to discover that they had been used as his material.

Galsworthy's estimate of how they would behave was probably accurate. Of all people who would have been expected to read the book, perhaps the most likely was Major Arthur; he was not the model for Soames Forsyte, but it was his marriage to Ada, and the unhappiness she found in it, that inspired the whole novel (and, indeed, to a degree created the whole novelist). But in fact, Major Arthur never did read *The Man of Property*: or so, at any rate, said his second wife, Wilhelmine. She herself, once she had learned of its bearing on her husband's first marriage, did out of curiosity read it. She thought it disgusting.

XIII

The publication of *The Man of Property*, on March 23, 1906, did not bring the recognition that it deserved. It was seen at once by most reviewers to be notable but none instantly perceived that it would come to rank in the main line of the English comic novel, or that it would add a household name to the language and contribute at least two portraits to the gallery of immortal English fictional characters. Conrad himself reviewed it for J. L. Garvin in the *Outlook*, sending to Galsworthy a letter of excuses for the article's inadequacy; years later, when Conrad was collecting his scattered essays for book publication, he tried to dodge recalling this one, declaring that he had never written anything about Galsworthy, and blaming himself for a lapse of memory when a copy of the *Outlook* article was placed before him.

The novel did not at that time make a great impression upon the public either. The sale of the 1906 edition came to only about 5,000 copies.

What it did do for Galsworthy, however, was to place him among the established and recognized novelists of his day. Little more than a year earlier he had been an obscure, unregarded writer, living a life of personal secrecy on a small unearned income. Now suddenly he was a man of inherited wealth who by his marriage had taken at least the first step towards rehabilitation from the scandal of the divorce case and whose name was securely known to all people interested in letters. As he himself later put it, "In 1906, before *The Man of Property* had appeared, I had been writing nearly eleven years without making a penny, or any name to speak of. *The Man of Property* had taken me nearly three years, but it *was* 'written'. My name was made; my literary independence assured; and my income steadily swollen."

In that same year he wrote his first completed play, *The Silver Box*, and at one stroke became the most discussed and controversial playwright of the year.

It was a remarkable emergence, and the picture of his whole life changed completely. He moved with Ada, now his wife, into the house he had acquired at 14 Addison Road, Kensington, with its garden backing on to Holland Park. With them went the spaniel dog, John (or Chris, or one of many other nicknames), which filled in their affections the place of a child, and which Galsworthy used as a prominent character in his next novel. They had not much company from their family or former friends (save, of course, from Galsworthy's two sisters), for they were still ostracized. There were a few literary circles in which they could move: the Garnetts and Conrad, and to some extent the Hueffers; W. H. Hudson, Gilbert Murray, E. V. Lucas, an acquaintance with Shaw and Harley Granville-Barker, and with H. G. Wells (though between Wells and Galsworthy there was always to be an instinctive antipathy, both personal and literary). Through Murray they were later to enter on a lifelong friendship with Barrie. But they had not many close friends, either old or new. Galsworthy was stiff and diffident with all but a very few people. Ada, more affected by the divorce and the scandal than she would admit, probably, even to herself, was developing ill-health. She suffered chiefly from either asthma or rheumatism, the one coming on as she recovered from an attack of the other, and from long and severe headcolds which both she and Galsworthy often elevated to the importance of "the 'Flue". She was, in the recollection of her intimates, a charming hostess when she had to be, but for long periods she retreated into an absorption in her illness, her husband's writing and her piano.

They soon found a remote country place to which they could still further retreat when they wished—Wingstone, the farmhouse on the edge of Dartmoor, where they had gone to provide Major Arthur with the evidence for his divorce proceedings. From the farmer, a solid Devonian named Endicott, they rented the whole of the front of the house, facing south —the part which had previously been reserved for summer lettings—and moved their own furniture in. The south front was long and low, with a veranda running its whole length, where Galsworthy could sit and write on sunny mornings. On the ground floor were the living-room into which a piano was put for Ada, a dining-room-cum-study; on the floor above, a little room in the centre, a bedroom on either side, and a room at the back which was too damp to be used. In front of the veranda a lawn sloped away into fields and then, across a small stream, to the moor. From the upper windows could be glimpsed the distant sea. In the back part of the house lived the farmer and his family; the domestic care of the Galsworthys fell to the farmer's wife, Mrs Endicott, a little lean and lively person, full of cheerfulness and humour. Behind the house the ordinary work and life of the farm went on, and there were stables for the Galsworthys' horses.

The place was reached by train to Newton Abbot, changing then for Bovey Tracey, and completing the journey by pony cart. Once arrived, life was simple, not to say primitive: no lighting or heating save candles and wood fires; no piped water, and therefore no bathroom—only tin baths, laboriously filled with hot water from cans.

It was the ideal retreat for a writer, a nature-lover and property-hater. It was, as he later put it, "richly sunk in all kinds of human and animal and bird life without any of the disgusting feeling that attaches to ownership. No servants—done for by the farmer's wife and niece and daughter—horses groomed by the farmer's stepson, no dogs of our own, but all the farm dogs running in and out as they like. All our food (nearly) grown on the spot. And all the time extraordinary goodwill; and the wonderful serene beauty; and air that has moor in it, a savour of the sea, and generally the crowning scent of woodsmoke. Garden beds, too, that have no wretched regularity, so that from day to day you don't know what's coming up, but which manage to be always pretty full. As to birds—those supreme joys—never was such a place for owls, cuckoos, buzzard hawks, and yaffles. Jays, too, and all song birds in proportion. . . . The people of these parts are pleasant to live among, when they know you, and know that you don't want to boss, or get anything out of them." The people to whom he referred were the farm people, for he and Ada were still, and for some time to come, shunned by the gentry.

To this remote place came few visitors—Gilbert Murray, Shaw and his wife driving across from Torquay, or Harley Granville-Barker. Galsworthy's life at Wingstone was mainly his writing and Ada. Writing, riding, walking; wood-smoke and candle-light; in the evening the piano softly and most beautifully played; and, before bed, always a step outside the door into the darkness, his invariable habit in the country, to stand in solitude for some minutes, listening, gazing at the sky.

By the opening of 1906, however, they had not as yet rented Wingstone and had spent the preceding winter at Bolt Head in Devon, where Galsworthy had attended to the proofs of *The Man of Property* and, at Edward Garnett's suggestion, started to write a play. He had the beginning of it in his bag when he returned to Addison Road in January 1906, and had finished it by March. But he was not yet paying much attention to plays. He was absorbed in the plan of writing two more novels to follow *The Man of Property*—*Christian Ethics II* and *III*—to complete his demonstration of the utter disharmony of the Christian religion with the English character. The second, begun under the title of *Danae*, was to portray a woman "unburdened with a moral sense".

As he came to write it, however, he diverged almost without volition from his plan. He did not as yet perceive that he had stumbled upon an alternative plan. All that happened was that the novel he was writing of the amoral woman became cumbersome, began to seem rather silly; whereas the minor characters commenced to grow into the foreground. He therefore abandoned *Danae* after a few chapters, and worked some of the material into *The Country House*. He had great difficulty in getting this novel started. About a quarter of it was drafted before *The Man of Property* was published, but at that point Galsworthy decided the thing was wrong, so he burned his manuscript and started again, working away at the new version at Wingstone in the spring and in London during the summer. He took it with him when he, Ada and old Mrs Galsworthy set off in July for a long tour of the Tyrol and returned with the book two-thirds done; by the end of November he had finished it. Once restarted, indeed, the book ran away with him, as he afterwards recorded, and was finished more swiftly than any of his novels.

The Country House was a gentler satire than *The Man of Property*. The story is about the disruption of the smug life of a Victorian country house by the amoral woman, Helen Bellew, with whom the squire's son, George Pendyce, is hopelessly in love, and over whom her husband is threatening the scandal of a divorce. But when he came to touch in the squire himself, the pompous, self-esteeming country gentleman, Horace Pendyce of Worsted Skeynes, the very Englishness of the man began to usurp the centre of the novel, for all the fun that Galsworthy poked at him. When he came to draw the portrait of Horace Pendyce's wife, who had spent thirty years of boredom in marriage without losing her gentleness of heart, and could be roused only to fight quietly, but invincibly, for her son's happiness, the satire faded almost entirely away. For all the simplicity of the portrait, Margery Pendyce is the most charming of all the women in Galsworthy's novels. So far as is known, there was no particular model for her; unless she were the mother he wished he had had.

There is enough social paraphernalia in the book, most of it furnished by Helen Bellew's sentimentally idealistic guardian, Gregory Vigil, railing at the absurdity, the injustice, the dishonesty and the indecency of the English laws of divorce, from which, of course, Galsworthy and Ada had recently suffered. There is passion of a not very convincing kind, for Galsworthy's amoral woman is a puppet from melodrama and George Pendyce, her lover, comes alive only on a race course. H. G. Wells's comment on Helen Bellew (in a curt, cutting letter to Galsworthy) is apt, "The bad woman you have seen across a room".

But in the country house itself the novel takes on that quality of sympathetic understanding that warms a satire and melts its edges. Galsworthy liked these people. They were the sort of people, as he went to great pains to discover, from whom he was himself descended on his mother's side—the gentry, a little crass perhaps, unimaginative, but staunchly English in a far more endearing way than were the Forsytes. The life in the country houses of late Victorian times was what he had most enjoyed in his youth, the contented emptiness of it, the leisure, the sports of the fields. Of all sports, shooting was that which he had most delighted in as a young man. It is true that he had given it up by the time he came to write of it. After a ten-year struggle with his conscience which lasted well into his twenties, it became plain to him that a man who, on principle, loathed cruelty and in fact loved animals, could not also take part in the slaughter on the moors. The conversion came, most inaptly, just when his spaniel John had been with him a year and was developing into a perfect gun dog. For six years thereafter, in deference to the spaniel's hereditary instincts, his master sent him each August to a Scottish shooting. He developed "a lovely nose and a perfect mouth, large enough to hold gingerly the biggest hare". Galsworthy, however, was never there to appreciate him. He had given up shooting as a sport.

But the memory remained and the old delight could not be kept from the tip of his J nib: "George felt the ground with his feet, and blew a speck of dust off his barrels, and the smell of the oil sent a delicious tremor darting through him. Everything, even Helen Bellew, was forgotten. Then in the silence rose a far-off clamour; a cock pheasant, skimming low, his plumage silken in the sun, dived out of the green and gold spinney, curled to the right, and was lost in the undergrowth. Some pigeons passed over at a great height. The tap-tap of sticks beating against trees began; then with a fitful rushing noise a pheasant came straight out. George threw up his gun and pulled. The bird stopped in mid-air, jerked forward and fell headlong into the grass sods with a thud. In the sunlight the dead bird lay, and a smirk of triumph played on George's lips. He was feeling the joy of life."

Had it not been for that whisper in the Gare du Nord about writing, had it not been indeed for Ada altogether, Galsworthy might so easily have been doing the same. Returning to his duty with a slight sigh, he went on to describe the agony of a wounded rabbit which had stolen out of a quivering wood and was dying: "It lay on its side on the slope of a tussock of grass, its hind legs drawn under it, its forelegs raised like the hands of a praying child. . . ." But even in that passage he could not forgo a swift, longing glance at "the keeper's cottage in the hollow, where late threads of crimson clung in the brown network of Virginia creeper, [and from which] rose a mist of wood smoke, dispersed upon the breeze". There was no sound except the far calling of men and beasts and birds that never quite dies of a country evening; some startled wood pigeons wheeled high above; and a gleam of sunlight stole down a covert to lay a burnish on the turned leaves. In *The Country House* he was writing of the privileged life which it had been the biggest wrench to give up and whose people he most respected of all his kind. Even in the savage portrait of the rector, the Rev. Hussell Barter, with his broad, red-brown face, his uncomplaining wife who presents him with a child every year, his narrowness of mind and the indifference with which, in the cause of morality, he precipitates a tragedy—even in Hussell Barter, in whom Galsworthy most gratuitously expressed his contempt for organized religion, there are touches to lessen the asperity, small strokes of sympathy and understanding. For he was a country parson.

The novel is more "written", as Galsworthy himself would have put it, than was *The Man of Property*; and for that reason is a lesser novel. There is a little too much evidence of the professional settling to a skilled job. Even in the scenes connected with the threatened divorce he seems to be making propaganda points rather than writing with anguish. The crisis of his life with Ada having passed, so had the fervour.

Now and then, too, the technique itself failed, usually in over-written sentimental scenes; that, for example, in which Horace Pendyce grapples with the news of his son's involvement in the divorce, while continually treading on the paws of his agitated and crawling spaniel, John. Like all his novels, too, this one is marred by his most irritating trick which was to scatter exclamation marks throughout his writing as though from an inexhaustible pepperpot! He used them, not only to mark an exclamation, but in place of a full-stop whenever he wanted emphasis—and sometimes in place of a semi-colon! —or even a comma! There are so many of them that, merci-

fully! the reading eye can learn to ignore them, to skip by them, though never to appreciate them except by avoidance! To pay attention to them is to make Galsworthy's books almost unreadable—there are so many of the d—d screamers! The samples inserted here can all be matched many times over in most of the novels. He kept up the habit throughout his life. It is almost his last novel which contains the superb example:
" '... "Shoot and be damned!"?...' "

When *The Country House* was published in March 1907, it was received with almost universal praise, though sales of the book did not very much exceed those of *The Man of Property*. More important to Galsworthy himself, however, was the direction in which *The Country House* had set his plans. The three-volume series intended to demonstrate the paganism of the English would not work. What Galsworthy now put in its place was a series of novels, each satirizing one section of contemporary society—by which he meant chiefly well-to-do society. He had already published two novels towards the series, dealing respectively with the materialism of the upper middle class in London, and the crass self-importance of the squirearchy. Two more were to come. He called the whole sequence "my long four-volume image of England's upper crust". The third, *Fraternity*, took for its subject the cultured æsthetic intellectuals of London, crammed with idealism but helpless when brought into actual contact with the masses around them, whose poverty they so greatly deplored in theory but of whom they had not the smallest understanding. The last novel, *The Patrician*, dissected the English aristocracy. These were the four main parts of the scheme, and though its seed had been planted in the earlier *The Island Pharisees*, there was a further flowering in the plays, and a weakened last fruit in a fifth novel, *The Freelands*, written as the Great War swept away the writer's subject-matter.

XIV

The times were favourable for such a project. England's Kiplingesque decade had died with the old Queen, and been followed by the Liberal upsurge which reached its height between 1906 and 1910. There is something in Galsworthy's belief that it was a revulsion from the Boer War which created the spirit of rebellion within him and loosed his novels; they fitted into the new spirit of the times. But this is only a superficial view of his motives and source-springs. He would have been no rebel had not the society to which he belonged thrust out Ada. Moreover, the satirical strength of *The Man of Property* diminished in each of the succeeding novels, the attack weakened and the serious interests of pure narrative became ever more important. For with each year that passed and with every success that Galsworthy scored, he brought Ada back more and more securely into the very society he was criticizing and in which his inherited money enabled him more and more easily to claim his place. The last vicious fling was at the aristocracy, for whom money held the least importance. When, in the turmoil of the war, his satiric impulse died away, it was because the destruction of the society he had attacked was also that of a rigid system of conventional morality which had excluded Ada.

In the spring and summer of 1907, when the climate was one of social reform—when, indeed, the foundations of the welfare state were about to be laid—Galsworthy turned to these exact themes, allied with a contempt for the ineffectiveness of the middle-class intellectuals among whom he lived. The roots of all this went down into his explorations as a young man of the London slums and his sense of guilt at the

comfort and wealth of his own lot. But the actual work began
with a sketch called "A Lost Dog", which was published in
the periodical, the *Nation*. It is simply a conversation with a
down-and-out in a London street at night, curiously recalling
the chance meeting with the Belgian tramp which began that
earlier work of introspection, *The Island Pharisees*. From this
one sketch, others followed—a young baker with tuberculosis
who faces unemployment with the certain knowledge that he
will be unable to provide for his wife and child; an old couple,
penniless after a lifetime of labour, who will starve rather than
go to the infirmary. The sketches are all written in the contemporary radical mood, a compound of pity and guilt, shy-
ing away from rational political thought or from the very
name of socialism. The tone is set by an old man in the title
essay, who has a job steering traffic past a steam-roller working in the road and muses in an innocent, half-baked sort of
way about necessary reform: slum women should be stopped
from incessant breeding (and half of the breeding is the result
of drink); all children should be fed by the State—a sixpenny
rate would do it, but nobody will give up his comforts. Side
by side with such sketches he placed several of the cosy life
of the wealthy middle-class Londoners, most of them self-
conscious little literary essays. In one, "Sport", he set the
sacrifice of birds in a Scottish shooting party alongside the
herding into a London police court of those other victims of
Edwardian masculine sport, the prostitutes. None of this,
obviously, was very profound, although when the sketches
were published in 1908 in a volume, *A Commentary*, they
aroused angry political criticism. They also deeply impressed
Galsworthy's new-found friend, Barrie, and from Conrad they
brought a renewed flow of exaggerated praise, though with
more sincerity than before. Perhaps this was because the
sketches of *A Commentary* were an emotional rather than an
intellectual reaction to the social problems which were then

occupying so much of the national scene, and therefore further removed from a course of action. Some of them were also preliminary sketches for his next novel; indeed, he started work on the novel when only two or three of the sketches had been written and returned to the composition of some more sketches whenever the long narrative flagged. The sketches were a notebook which he kept going alongside his novel and to which he could turn to jot down some theme, some character, that could prove useful in the work proper.

He began the novel under the title *Shadows*, which exactly declares its purpose; he abandoned that title only when he found it was to be used on somebody else's book. He then gave his own the more satiric title of *Fraternity*—that brotherhood between the well-to-do intellectuals of London and the dwellers in the neighbouring slums which, although perhaps sincerely desired, was never to be anything but frustrated, congealed, impossible.

It is set entirely in Kensington; either in that select, artistic, wealthy Kensington that lies about the High Street, Campden Hill and Holland Park, or in the slums brooding on the other side of the main road towards Notting Hill or beyond Cromwell Road towards Fulham. In the wealthier half live the Dallisons—delicate, sensitive people, whose very dog, Miranda, an overbred little bulldog bitch, loathes and shrinks from life. Hilary Dallison is an æsthetic writer of troubled, humane instincts and independent means whose wife Bianca, a painter in the modern style, introduces into the house a young girl from the slums as a model for her painting, "Shadow", a dim picture of a girl beneath a London street-lamp, stretching out her hands. When the work is over, it seems intolerable that the girl should return to the complete poverty from which she came. Bianca's father, an elderly, ascetic, half-crazed, retired professor named Stone, who is composing a vast never-to-be-published masterpiece of satiric philosophy, gives her some copying work to do. Hilary regards her merely with sympathetic pity, but at the least hint of this most innocent attraction, his wife quarrels with him in a civilized and refined way and they cease to be "on terms".

In the slums there is another man—a street trader, a vigorous animal with wretched wife and sickly, dying children —whose life is also being destroyed by his desire for the little model. The girl herself, predatory, sees in Hilary the chance of escape from her poverty—a chance which she misses by offering herself to him a little too freely, a little too soon, with the coarseness of a kiss that outrages his sensibility and thrusts him back into the tragedy of frustration, futility and the inability to take any sort of action.

Conrad, to whom Galsworthy turned with this particular manuscript (feeling, perhaps, that Garnett was not quite the man for it), responded with fervour. When he had read it, he asked himself "whether we have not here a writer in the direct descent of the great tradition of the English art of Novelwriting—I mean the highest tradition". All one night he sat up, slowly and painfully writing sixteen pages of analysis and discussion of the book, pointing out some small defect of technique here, making some minor suggestion for a different treatment there; and, as everyone whose advice Galsworthy sought on a manuscript always seemed to do, suggesting a different ending. He wrote, as he said, in an almost fierce affection for his work. This aroused from Galsworthy the customary unhappy letter of explanation and defence of his own viewpoint, followed soon after by a careful rewriting of the parts criticized. He altered, for example, the ending, though not in the manner that Conrad had suggested.

What he had at last was a strong novel—probably the most neglected of his major works—in which the various strains of his writing were curiously intermixed. There is satire of prosperous, intellectual Kensington; of well-to-do women

devoting themselves, under the pretence of charity, to inter-
fering in other people's lives; of the irresolute feeling of guilt
with which one of the Dallison wives buys from an expensive
shop in the High Street a dress which she cannot resist, although she murmurs to herself that she ought not to do so
"with all this distress about". There is the liberal mind, deeply
worried by the misery of others, searching anxiously for some
amelioration of it which will not disturb the organization of
society unduly, but will suffice to fend off the vague hints of
coming violence and trouble. This aspect of the book was
what drew the heaviest criticism when it was published in
1909; not surprisingly, of course, when reform was in the
atmosphere, the socialists were at least a threat and a forebod-
ing, and the government were preparing to bring into existence those early measures of social security which would
ameliorate the very miseries which the two books, A Commentary and Fraternity, set forth. For this reason the Saturday
Review could castigate Fraternity as a dangerous and
revolutionary book, "an insidious and embittered attack on
our social system". This topical aspect obscured at the time the
failure of the novel to portray the slum life of London in any
real sense. Everything was observed and reported through the
eyes of a perpetual slum visitor, a social worker. Galsworthy,
for all his longing to sympathize with his fellow creatures,
was never able for one moment to step across his own class
frontier and portray the life of the poor from within. He never
comprehended the humour and liveliness of slum life, as, for
supreme example, Dickens had done. Galsworthy's slum-
dwellers are drab and wretched, their lives are continually
sordid and mean; the rain, one feels, never ceases over North
Kensington (though the sun is shining on Campden Hill), and
nobody existing on the wrong side of the Cromwell Road
sparkles with a moment of natural gaiety or even of sensual
pleasure.

The political resentment aroused by *Fraternity* obscured its attempt at the classic theme of intellectual atrophy, of the inability to act because of moral doubts and mind searchings. In the Dallisons, with their futility, their frustrations, their sensitivity, Galsworthy was trying to show how the intellectual life of the nation had been sapped and rendered impotent by a half-century of money and ease, so that even that section of his own class with whom he had most natural sympathy had grown enfeebled and incapable of taking a part in the future—even in its own future. The diagnosis was wrong, as was to be shown conclusively in 1914; but the figures of the novel, taken out of their contemporary setting, have in them a timelessness, an element of enduring humanity, which Conrad perceived to be the nearest that Galsworthy had got (or, in fact, ever would get) to the subtle, enervated characters of the Russian novels which he had at first taken as his model and his literary ideal. All the comparisons in Conrad's long letters of discussion and advice on *Fraternity* are with the Russian novels. This intensity of feeling may have been because, for the first time since *The Island Pharisees*—for the first time, therefore, in his literary maturity—Galsworthy was writing, not about Ada, not about his family, but about himself. In the timidity and deep shyness of the writer Dallison is the self-questioning, the guilty consciousness of his own good fortune in comparison to that of others and the hesitant radicalism of the writer Galsworthy.

This was not a mood which he carried forward into the fourth and last of his novels of "the image of England's upper crust", *The Patrician*, which he largely wrote in the spring and summer of 1910, with much rewriting in the autumn. Here, putting hesitations aside, he was the professional novelist in full power of composition, setting his scenes, marshalling his characters and creating a fictional world that was inevitably slightly false, artificial, manufactured.

131

He used once more the theme derived from Ada, that of the woman entrapped in a loveless marriage. Audrey Noel, often throughout the narrative called Anonyma, is a woman of unknown antecedents living in a remote part of the country, with whom Miltoun, a young nobleman destined for a great political career in the manner of his house, falls in love. The mystery that Anonyma hides is that she is the wife of a clergyman, from whom she has separated since they cannot live together, but from whom she can never expect to obtain a divorce. Miltoun's family and in particular his aristocratic grandmother, Lady Casterley, fight ruthlessly against his passionate determination to give up his career, his duty towards his country, for the woman with whom he is in love; and in the end they win. Anonyma goes abroad and the austere Miltoun, broken of the one assuagement of his ascetic nature, returns to the austere task of government. Alongside Miltoun's story runs that of his sister, Barbara, who is attracted, though not passionately, by a young radical named Courtier, devoted to lost causes, who seems, curiously, to have been suggested by H. W. Nevinson. (When this was later pointed out to Nevinson, he wrote to Galsworthy to tell him he found the portrait—if such it were—flattering; but to add staunchly that the causes he had advocated from time to time—the Boers, the Angola slaves, Russian Revolutionists, Indian Nationalists, Finland, Suffragettes—were all winning causes, or soon would be. Galsworthy replied that Courtier was not so much a portrait of Nevinson as a portrait in spite of Nevinson; that is, he was a man of Nevinson's type, and the mere fact that Galsworthy knew him in real life had impeded the drawing. It had been far easier, he assured him, to model Miltoun slightly upon Lord Hugh Cecil, since he had never, in fact, met that nobleman in the flesh.)

The happiest touches in *The Patrician* are little scenes of English country life, put in with the quiet felicity of a Morland painting, though marred here and there by the attempt to render dialect phonetically which Galsworthy persisted in making, and almost never successfully pulled off. But for all this feeling of Englishness, it is not a remarkable novel. The impulse derived from his love for Ada was dying away and the satire which grew from his anger was fading. This he knew. He declared that the diminution of satire throughout the four upper-crust novels was of deliberate policy, in order to allow more room for beauty; what it really allowed more room for was narration of a story. Moreover, the last phrase of *The Patrician*—"all are in bond to their own natures, and what a man has most desired shall in the end enslave him"—applied more aptly to himself than he can certainly have understood. What he most desired was a place of eminence and respect for Ada and himself in the society in which he had grown up, certainly not to destroy that society. In his collected-edition preface, written years later, to *The Country House*, he refers to all four of his "class" novels thus, "Sensitiveness to the blind spots of the upper classes used to bring this Author the reputation of a revolutionary, among those 'weeklies' which champion the upper dog—a quaint conceit concerning one of the least political of men. The constant endeavour of his pen has merely been to show Society that it has had luck; and, if those who have had luck behaved as if they knew it, the chances of revolution would sink to zero." The rebellion was soon over.

That he was uneasy about *The Patrician* is evident from the extra nervous care which he took to obtain the opinions of his friends on the manuscript. As always, he needed somebody whom he could respect to reassure him constantly while he was in the course of composition. Ada did so day by day, almost word by word. But this was not enough. Directly any sizeable amount of the book was written, the manuscript had to go off to, in effect, some tutor who could point out where he might be going wrong and arouse him to an indignant defence of his own work followed by a compliant revision.

On this occasion he first chose Gilbert Murray, who was not only a friend, with all those qualities of high academic and literary distinction that sufficed to endorse his opinions, but had also married into the class which Galsworthy was here trying to depict. Murray, who was eventually to get the book dedicated to him for his pains, took great trouble over it, reading and re-reading it chapter by chapter and offering copious criticisms and suggestions. His first major objection was that when Miltoun went off with Mrs Noel, the scandal would be such that he would be bound to lose his parliament-ary seat at the next election; and most men would either resign at once, or, at least, cease to attend the House. All the spiritual struggle of Part II of the book would, therefore, not arise, be-cause even if he did not want to resign, "he would jolly well have to".

This, naturally, was a great blow to the author. Surely it could not be that the very structure upon which he had lab-oured so thoroughly was unsound! In his first letter to Mur-ray he writhed and twisted in his arguments to support his narrative but within twenty-four hours he was already con-sidering a complete recasting of the second part of the book. "My lazy spirit and rather tired head recoil—but, after all, if I get a clear vision I shall have to go for it; and there's a good deal I might save—I think—of what's written. Send the beastly thing back. . . . Damn! Never did I get through a novel without one of these bitings of the dust."

While he was making his revisions, he was also going out of his way to meet as many aristocrats as he could, declaring that he needed further study. His bag of titles at that time was impressive, and he listed them in his notebook-diary as among those whose acquaintance he then made: "Mr and Mrs Asquith, Lord Morley, Lord and Lady Ilchester, Lord and Lady

Ridley, Arthur and Gerland Balfour, Sidney Webb and Mrs Webb"—something of a let-down there—"Lloyd George, Sir Charles Dilke, Lord McDonnell", and so on and so on, ending with "the Duchesses of Sutherland and Marlborough". He added, "Generally speaking, rather 'after' patricians at this time. Met a good many. Revivifying College and other recollections of them."

Fortified by this research, he laboured at the manuscript, finishing the first draft while on a holiday visit to Scotland, at an hotel recommended by J. M. Barrie. He despatched it to Murray, "considerably trembling", and then he and Ada went off to stay with his sister Mabel and her family, who had taken a house for the summer near Padstow in Cornwall. There he awaited Murray's verdict. But all was well. "It is very, very beautiful," wrote Murray, "I am clear about that, and also clear that you have got it right...."

Thus encouraged, Galsworthy sent a typed copy of the manuscript to his true mentor, Edward Garnett, and the ensuing comedy of letters continued for some three months. Garnett did not like the book. In the first paragraph of his first letter about it he explained exactly why: "You don't know these people well enough to produce an original and really convincing picture."

It was a perfectly correct criticism of the book, bluntly expressed. For that, of course, all the more wounding. In a postscript Garnett casually added that Galsworthy's attitude towards the class he was writing about, the aristocrats, had "an upward slant" to it. It was all guesswork, all done from the outside.

Galsworthy, contriving with obvious difficulty to remain unruffled, civilized—even civil as usual—protested that Garnett was starting with the idea that he could not know those people and then making everything square with that. As a matter of fact, Galsworthy told him in a dignified way, he *did* know a lot of these people: "Half my set at Oxford belonged to them. I have met them here and there, and especially of late"; as, indeed, he deliberately had. As for the "upward slant", with all its implications of snobbery (neither of them using that word), it was a quite unfair reproach. It was simply because the aristocrat excited him to such animosity that he had deliberately used favourable specimens in *The Patrician*, in order not to give way to that animosity. He was grateful to Garnett for writing what he felt, for it must have been very unpleasant. (There is no indication in Garnett's letters that he suffered any distress at all.) "By the way," ended Galsworthy, "let us not mention this unfortunate book again."

This stirred the controversy into much fuller correspondence. Put the book aside for two months, begged Garnett. He spoke as a friend to whom Galsworthy's reputation was dear. He understood, of course, the reason for his attitude towards the aristocrats. He simply wanted to be fair to them; which is why the presentation of them had turned out to be too deferential. That must have stung. But Galsworthy returned a rather conciliatory reply, promising to work over the book, as he always did, in the interval before it should be published. For there was already stirring in him the uneasiness, which he invariably felt under criticism, particularly by Garnett, lest the critic might be right.

Thus encouraged, Garnett got down to a detailed analysis of the novel. Point by point he dealt with it, like a schoolmaster giving a lesson.

That was too much. Galsworthy had accepted the tuition in earlier years, but now he rebelled. All the irritation he had for so long felt about Garnett (while at the same time valuing his advice) came welling up in a huge letter which he wrote at Wingstone in the middle of September: "Forgive this outpouring, dear boy, but I have always suffered a little from a sense of injustice at your hands—ever since I read an extract from your report on *Jocelyn* (which should never have been sent to me) to the effect that I should never be an artist but always look at life as from the windows of a Club."

That was how much it had rankled. It was twelve years since Galsworthy had seen that chance remark by Garnett, then reading for Fisher Unwin. All those years he had restrained his resentment. Now he let fly: "Book by book, I've always a little felt that you *unconsciously* grudged having to recede from that position. That, with your strong, and in those days still more set belief in your own insight (which is very great), you had summed me up and could not be wrong. I have always felt that I am deeper, more fluid, perhaps broader than you think. Being dumb, I've never said so— but perhaps you'll forgive me once in these ten years (and more) saying out my feeling. In fact I've always felt that I was contending with a *parti pris* perpetually confirmed in you, whenever we are together, by my slowness of tongue and manner. You say 'This book is not you,' but this seems to suggest that you have fixed me as something special, definite, narrow. This is what I always feel in you. 'Jack is so-and-so, *et voilà tout!*' It is the habit, I suppose, of the critical mind, which has to form its judgment on definite things, to deny the possibility of change or growth until that change or growth has utterly fulfilled itself."

When Garnett got that he gave a good-humoured chuckle and yielded: "Damn you! Of course I'm unjust to you. Haven't you gone and done wonders, all along the line, in fiction and the drama, and left us gaping and scratching our heads. Of course we're pleased to get a knife into you, when we can, and find out that you are also vulnerable and mortal!"

He had forgotten all about that early summing up of Galsworthy the Clubman, but he freely admitted it was absurd: "No, my dear boy, the diagnosis of the *parti pris* in me with which you contend is different. It's like the attitude of a race-

137

course hawker to a surprising animal that has been a 'dark horse', and has gone on winning all the Cups afterwards! 'Gawd bless you, that 'orse came out of Mr Bindley's stables. I knowed where 'e came from; they used to feed 'im on turnip mash.' "

Then he diffidently admitted his jealousy of Galsworthy—jealousy of his success, jealousy of his wealth: "It's a good bit *circumstances*, like houses and suits of clothes."

As for *The Patrician*, no doubt Galsworthy was right. He yielded absolutely. Galsworthy did know what he was about. All the same . . .

Yet, with that, the dispute between them, that had so nearly uncovered ugliness, was over. They went on arguing over points of detail, points of difference, but there was no more animosity, hidden or disclosed. All the time Galsworthy was revising and rewriting, putting into the novel much of the advice that he had bridled at receiving. When it was nearly done he admitted, "I've benefited greatly by your sensitive perceptions; but confound you—you took me the wrong way altogether; and you really ought not to have accused me of doing such a fatuous thing as start a job of this sort without knowing my ground." That was what had most truly hurt—the "upward slant". To satisfy himself that he really did know a lot of noblemen, he told Garnett, he had been counting up "the aristocrats pure I've known or observed at close quarters—many in the last three years—as far as I can remember, they come to about 130". Moreover, he enclosed a list; and he could have doubled it in length, he assured Garnett, by including people who, though not actually titled, might just as well be styled aristocrats.

By mid-November, when the revision was almost completed, Galsworthy admitted to Garnett that he had rewritten practically every passage which Garnett had queried. But he still maintained that he had not altered the essence of the book.

Most perceptively he then added that "this book, like *The M. of P.*, *The C. H.* and *Fraternity* is simply the criticism of one half of myself by the other, the halves being differently divided according to the subjects. It is not a piece of social criticism—they none of them are. If it's anything it's a bit of spiritual examination".

And thus, with the best-selling and most popular of all his novels at that time, Galsworthy came to the end of that phase of his writing which was, in effect, that phase of his life in which he and Ada had suffered and he had struck back with his pen. He had not had the courage or perhaps the perception to tell Garnett that the two halves of himself which were warring in those novels were that which defied the world on Ada's behalf and that which accepted the world as good, right and just, for all its strictures upon her. Or perhaps it was simply that, now he and Ada were beginning to be comfortably re-established in the society of their time, he had simply forgotten.

XV

To treat only of these "class" novels published between 1904 and 1911 is to give, however, a scanty idea of the busyness of Galsworthy's life and the influence he had come to wield. For a man may go on writing excellent novels, year after year, and gain little but indifferent respect, yet one successful play will thrust him to prominence; though later it may be evident that the play was a transitory, topical, dating sort of thing and the true worth lay in the long prose narratives.

When Galsworthy began writing his first completed play, *The Silver Box*, on a holiday in Devon, *The Man of Property* had not yet been published and he was still struggling with the early chapters of *The Country House*. Garnett's suggestion that he should attempt a play probably came simply as a respite from the more arduous task. Naturally Garnett was shown the draft of the manuscript and he suggested a good many improvements, even some of the lines. They also had their usual argument about the conception of one or two of the characters—Galsworthy rejected Garnett's wider suggestion that the whole thesis of the play was faulty and that it might be better to start afresh.

The writing was finished in less than six weeks. Garnett's idea had been from the start that the play should be aimed at the Court Theatre, where Bernard Shaw and Harley Granville-Barker were establishing the new school of dramatists of the real. The play was therefore despatched to Granville-Barker on a Saturday at the end of March 1906. Both he and Shaw read it on the Sunday, both strongly approved of it, and on the Monday Granville-Barker accepted it for production in the autumn—at first for matinées only, but later for an evening run. There is a curious parallel between all this and the swift acceptance at the same theatre, some half-century later, of John Osborne's *Look Back in Anger*, with which a more recent school of new dramatists of the real was consolidated. There is also a parallel in the receptions given to these two plays, fifty years or so apart, each striking vigorously, within its contemporary limitations, at the established society of its day. "It is not a cheerful play," wrote one critic of *The Silver Box*, "but if you neglect to see it you will probably miss seeing a play which will continually be quoted when the new school of dramatists has been established. If prophecy upon stage matters were not such an idle form of amusement, I would indulge in wild imaginings concerning the effect *The Silver Box* is likely to have upon the theatre of the future." Wrote another, "Probably by not thinking about the matter at all, Mr Galsworthy has evolved a method of his own for presenting life on the stage that is completely successful. . . . When its author wrote it he was thinking of life, not of the theatre, and though he never forgot that he was writing for performance, he never allowed himself to sacrifice truth to mere stage effect or to shirk the situation as it would happen in life for the situation that the old-fashioned playwright had found to be effective on the stage. Hence the extraordinary success of his play."

He could not, however, have been dubbed an angry young man, even had phraseology of that kind been then in fashion, for by the time his first completed attempt at a play had made this notable mark on the theatre, Galsworthy was in his fortieth year.

What gave the play most of its impact was the third Act. In *The Silver Box*, which he had started under the title of *The Cigarette Box*, this article itself, resting on a tray with a whisky bottle and siphon in the dining-room of the London house of a wealthy Liberal member of Parliament, symbolizes property. Jack Barthwick, the dissolute young son of the family, returning home drunk after a late evening with a prostitute (from whom, in pique, he has snatched her handbag), brings into the house the equally drunken, out-of-work husband of the charwoman who works there. This man Jones, smouldering with anger at the destitution into which society has forced him, takes in spite, rather than steals, the silver box. But when it is missed the following day it is his wife, who has cleaned the room, who is suspected. When the box is found in their tenement room, they are both arrested. Only then does it become clear to the elder Barthwick, the unctuous, posturing Liberal, and to his conventionally intolerant wife, that the charge which they can no longer drop against the Joneses may well bring into the open the scandal of their son's behaviour towards the prostitute. In the last Act, therefore, which is set in a London police court, all the power of money and the forces of privilege, with which the magistrate inevitably sympathizes, are used in the neatest quietest way, to put Jones into gaol and leave his wife to face the world with her children in complete destitution, so that the son of a man of affluence shall not be in the least exposed. The thing is done with brutality, hypocrisy and cynicism. Once Jones, shouting with rage, has been safely thrust from the courtroom, Barthwick's solicitor has a quiet word with the reporter in the Press box, young Jack Barthwick walks out with a swagger, and his father, to whom Mrs Jones makes a humble appeal for help, hesitates, but then shamefacedly refuses her and hurries away.

Some of the success of *The Silver Box* doubtless derived from the acting, for the cast was notable. Edmund Gwenn and Lewis Casson had minor parts. Sydney Fairbrother played the prostitute, Irene Rooke was Mrs Jones, Norman McKinnell her husband, and (as a reminder of how long ago it was) the part of the dissolute young man went to A. E. Matthews.

Even in the direction of the performance Galsworthy had some share, for he dropped easily into the knowledgeable manner of a man of the theatre, discussing with Granville-Barker subtle considerations of casting, and coming away from rehearsals, which he assiduously attended, with professional-sounding comments on the acting. The rehearsals in themselves were a delight. At one of them Shaw came up to tell him he thought the play "very fine". But when at last it was produced at the Court Theatre on September 25, and the praise flowed in—even H. G. Wells was complimentary—Galsworthy suddenly felt uncertain and lost. To young Ralph Mottram, upon whose book of early poems he was then giving advice, he confided, "The play seems to have struck a good many people. The odd thing is I can't tell in the least what it's like. I lost one of my senses during rehearsals, but whether it was the sense of smell or not I don't know. I can't judge, anyway."

It was a mood that seems to have persisted, for his next play, *Joy*, was a sentimental piece of nonsense, set on a country-house lawn of a summer's day. All the sincerity, truthfulness, courage and animosity which he had brought to the writing of *The Silver Box* had evaporated. The play was produced, though at the Savoy Theatre, not the Court; and, of course, it flopped.

Meanwhile Galsworthy had become engrossed in another aspect of the theatre. Garnett had written a play, *The Breaking Point*, which was censored by the Lord Chamberlain, that archaic Court official who had hampered the English theatre for centuries, and still does. Garnett, helpless and in a rage, turned to Galsworthy—as a man of reputation and of wealth —to urge that he should organize a protest by contemporary writers. There had already that year been an attack on the iniquity of the censorship by William Archer, the critic. Then, in October, Granville-Barker's play, *Waste*, was censored.

This was enough. Galsworthy brought in Gilbert Murray, persuading him over dinner at Addison Road to enlist Barrie, and the three of them drafted a letter which was circulated to all writers of consequence in the country, and signed by seventy-one of them. The Prime Minister was compelled by the strength of the list to promise that a deputation should be received; and it was. Nothing followed. The authors then had a Bill drafted, and it was introduced into Parliament in 1908 with, of course, no effect.

In the following year Shaw's play, *Blanco Posnet*, was censored; and, later in that year, his *Press Cuttings*. Galsworthy, who throughout had led the agitation, came out with a pamphlet, *A Justification of the Censorship of Plays*. The sarcasm was somewhat heavy, the satire a little obvious, but it had its effect as the culmination of the campaign which he had begun, and in which the voice of literary England was sounding irritably. A Parliamentary Committee was conceded. It began to sit in the August of 1909, and heard evidence. Galsworthy's, delivered in dignified terms, concentrated on the deterrent, to men of letters having something significant to say, from choosing the dramatic form at all. When other forms of literary expression were not similarly hampered, they would not choose to work for the stage, where they regarded this "irresponsible Censorship . . . this arbitrary power, lodged in the hands of a single person, chosen we do not know why or how, to mutilate or bar our plays, in deference to we do not know what, as a standing insult to our good feeling, good taste, and sense of duty to the Public".

The Committee deliberated, published an ineffectual Report a few months later, and nothing further was done. But Galsworthy had tasted the power which can be exerted in public affairs by a literary reputation, even in England. It was a different sort of power from that obliquely wielded by a writer in the course of his work. The successful novelist could to

144

some extent influence the public view of manners, perhaps even, over a long period, change the climate of public opinion on the organization of society in general. But here, in this campaign against the Censorship, he had stirred up opinion directly and forced public authority to take specific action on a subject which was not merely of literary interest but was supposed to concern primarily the public morals. It is true that the campaign had not succeeded. Years later, Galsworthy felt he could claim that thereafter the Censorship had been exercised more sensibly; but this was far more probably due to the change wrought by the Great War in the whole attitude to morality than to the abortive efforts of the writers in 1909. Nevertheless the purely literary campaign had succeeded in compelling the authorities to some sort of placatory action. To that extent the power of the pen seemed to be as actual and visible, though of course nothing like as strong, as the power of money; it had an agreeable Forsytean flavour to it. The man who had attacked property and privilege could, for that very reason, have a say in public affairs. The rebel could exert authority. It all accorded well with Galsworthy's basic desire to restore himself, and therefore Ada, to that established respectability which he had assailed for spiting her. The former social outcast could, by the use of his pen, exert the same sort of influence, and be listened to with the same sort of deference, as could the politician or the barrister.

In the meantime, however, he was engaged upon another play, *Strife*, which certainly expressed a view on matters of public importance—on, that is, the growing ugliness of industrial relationships between master and men—but which had no direct, campaigning purpose and advocated no particular action. Galsworthy himself maintained, indeed, that the strike at a tin-plate works which provides the material of the play was only a convenient setting for his theme, which was the clash of extremists and their inevitable doom. He had begun work on it while staying at Lyme Regis in February 1908, continued at it during the following month when he moved on to Littlehampton, and finished it, in rough at least, by the end of April, on a visit to Westerham. That was about the speed at which he wrote his plays and that, also, the sort of restless wandering which he endured while writing.

He did not write *Strife* in reaction to the reception of his sentimental *Joy*, since in fact he had finished it in rough some six months before *Joy* was produced. But it had to wait, in the first place, until the earlier production had taken place; and then had to find a manager who would put it on after *Joy* had so damaged the new playwright's reputation. That took more than a year, and several managements declined. At last Charles Frohmann took the risk, presenting it for six matinées at the Duke of York's Theatre in March 1909. It was so instantly and vividly successful that it was transferred to evening performances at the Haymarket, where it played to full houses until previous engagements of some members of the cast, which included Lillah McCarthy (then married to Granville-Barker), compelled the run to end. Incidentally, it was the play with which the Liverpool Repertory Theatre was founded.

Galsworthy's friends and literary advisers had already assured him that *Strife* would be the play to make his name; he had sent the manuscript round and about for opinions, and Garnett had come up with some valuable suggestions, to several of which the author at once raised his usual insuperable objections. The correspondence, however, was short and not in the least heated. Conrad, on being given the play to read, had responded with "the murmurs against *Joy* shall be drowned in such a shout around *Strife* as this country has not heard for a hundred years or more. You've only got to sit tight and watch your glory approaching". So, allowing for exaggeration, it proved. The London critics acclaimed the play: Archer headed his notice in the *Nation*, "Mr Gals-

146

worthy Arrives". There was even a private note from the President of the Board of Trade, "I enjoyed and admired your play *Strife*. It is a fine piece of work which will long survive the silly chatter of the day.—Yours very truly, Winston S. Churchill." But not even that can have counted for more than the estimate of *The Times's* critic, who declared, "If we are not mistaken, when an artist of Mr Galsworthy's high endeavour, mental equipment and technical skill writes a play like *Strife*, he has done much more than write a play; he has rendered a public service." Nothing could have warmed Galsworthy more than that acceptance by authority of his reinstatement.

Indeed, rendering public services was precisely what he now conceived of himself as doing. He once, in later years, drew up a list of causes which he had actively supported and advocated. It ranges from divorce law reform, the establishment of a minimum wage in sweated industries, woman's suffrage and slum clearance, to such questions as prohibition of children on the theatrical stage, docking of horses' tails and advocacy of the three-year average system for income tax. Rendering public services became of such importance to him that he devoted himself untiringly to examining abuses and pursuing reforms. There is an entry a little later in the notebook-diary which he and Ada jointly kept, that reads, during a journey in Switzerland, "First sight of Geneva. J. went over a slaughterhouse there, struck him as pretty good, better than anything we have, which is saying little."

XVI

The particular campaign upon which he was engaged in 1909
was the reform of the system of solitary confinement of convicts in the prisons. From Wingstone farmhouse on the edge
of Dartmoor he had always been uneasily aware of the brooding prison. He was a genuinely compassionate man, the simple
idea of other people's misery distressed him unduly and he
truly wished to assuage it. In a book as early as *The Island
Pharisees* there is a scene outside Princetown prison, this
"lugubrious stone cage". Shelton, who represented the youthful Galsworthy, scans the walls with morbid fascination, and
reflects that "this, then, was the system by which men en-
forced the will of the majority, and it was suddenly borne in
on him that all the ideas and maxims which his Christian
countrymen believed themselves to be fulfilling daily were
stultified in every cellule of the social honeycomb. Such teach-
ings as 'He that is without sin amongst you' had been pronounced unpractical by peers and judges, bishops, statesmen,
merchants, husbands—in fact, by every truly Christian person in the country."

In September 1907, Galsworthy penetrated inside Dartmoor
gaol, and was so moved to distress by what he saw that he
began to devote himself to the abolition of solitary confinement, at that time imposed for nine months on habitual
criminals and for lesser periods on others, though even star
class convicts had to serve three months' solitary. He got into
touch with various reforming organizations and with certain
Members of Parliament who were sympathetic to his views,
and his first assault upon the system, other than two brief

sketches, was a long open letter to the Home Secretary, which the *Nation* published in two parts. This set off the whole liberal press—and, indeed, later the conservative press too. Galsworthy, leading the campaign, was put into touch with the head of the Prison Commission, Sir Evelyn Ruggles-Brise, and was thus enabled to visit other prisons. He did so both exhaustively and exhaustingly; the visit to Lewes gaol lasted for two days, during which he interviewed sixty prisoners at length. He wrote memoranda to the Prison Commission and to the Home Secretary and conducted the agitation so effectively that in September 1909 solitary confinement was reduced for all classes of prisoner to what had previously been the minimum period of three months.

While managing the public campaign, however, Galsworthy had also been composing a play, *Justice*, upon the theme of crime and disproportionate punishment, which went into the closed cell of a prison and showed a man in the torments of solitary confinement. He wrote it at his usual speed during his usual restless travels: six weeks in London and Ilkley during which he finished the first two Acts, and a week at Scarborough during which he wrote the third (the fourth was completed later in the year at Wingstone). He wrote it, too, while his other work was in full flow. In the early months of 1909 he also finished another play, the somewhat indifferent *The Eldest Son* (which was held over to make room for *Justice*) and a silly little musical whimsy which was produced at Manchester; he had started work on yet another play which he laid aside for a following year. This, too, was the year in which he wrote most of his novel, *The Patrician*, as well as a considerable body of lesser work. The composition naturally entailed, in addition, the usual anxious correspondence with those of his friends whose opinion he sought on his manuscripts. The chief consultant for *Justice* was Gilbert Murray, who was comfortingly enthusiastic.

When the play was produced at the Duke of York's Theatre in February 1910 it had an astonishing reception. Long after the final curtain had fallen on the first night, the gallery audience stayed in the theatre shouting for the author and refusing to leave until he should appear. In fact he was not in the house. The management tried every device to clear the theatre, including turning out all the lights, but the audience remained, calling enthusiastically, "We want Galsworthy", until nearly midnight, when Granville-Barker came on and persuaded them at last to disperse. The dramatic critics were equally complimentary next morning and letters of praise arrived from known and unknown people alike. "An intense piece of truth," wrote John Masefield; "it may have a great, perhaps an immense result upon our national attitude to crime. Good God, it is a revelation." From H. G. Wells came, "*Justice*, so far as the question of art goes, just establishes and vindicates you. I've always opposed myself to your very austere method hitherto. I've not liked a sort of cold hardness in much of your work, but since it leads you at last to the quite tremendous force of the play—well, I give in."

A theatre publicity man, had there been such persons in 1910, might well have admired the skill with which Galsworthy's campaign throughout the previous year against the evil of solitary confinement had stirred up enthusiasm for his play. But, of course, no such unworthy motive had occurred to him; that would have been quite outside his whole concept of behaviour, of art, of probity. Indeed, he was to some extent aggrieved because the emphasis on the play's propaganda qualities had, in his opinion, obscured its dramatic and artistic merits and the tragic nature of its true theme.

As propaganda, however, there could be no doubt of its success. Winston Churchill, recently appointed Home Secretary, was known to have been moved by it. Galsworthy therefore sent him a letter which initiated a long correspond-ence, begging him to "strike a crushing blow at a custom which continues to darken our humanity and good sense", and to abolish or at least further to ameliorate the system of solitary confinement which would remain even after the re-forms already granted had been put into effect. Churchill replied that he was in entire sympathy with Galsworthy's general mood, and had given instructions for the question to be brought before him without delay. When he had studied it, he wrote again to Galsworthy, telling him that the Home Office in general considered his portrayal of the prison scenes in *Justice* to be unfair, and making, among others, the point that it was essential not to make prison so little of a punish-ment as to leave on the mind of the victim of a crime a sense of aggrievement.

Galsworthy leaped into a reply that he had never doubted the good faith with which justice was administered or the humanity of the administration. He, like Churchill, greatly admired Sir Evelyn Ruggles-Brise, the chief of the Prison Com-mission (who, as always with the leaders of that admirable body, had in fact been far ahead of public opinion, and was largely responsible for the institution of such major reforms as the Borstal system). Nevertheless, the system of solitary confinement did appear to him dreadful and unnecessary, and he maintained with dignity that what he had written in his play was true: "Solitary confinement is a dumb thing; it can-not speak for itself; it is a long slow dragging misery, whose worst moments are necessarily and utterly hidden from our eyes. I have given it a tongue *for once*—surely that is not unfair. For it is my conviction that it is only because this thing is dumb that it has been kept on as part of our penal sys-tem. . . . This play was not written by me in any wanton spirit. It has been nothing but pain from beginning to end. It has cost me much peace of mind. I have written it, believing that what I have seen and thought and felt ought to be made known, and that I should not be true to myself or my art, and cowardly into the bargain, if I had turned my back on the task."

To such a letter Churchill warmly responded. He would never question Galsworthy's perfect sincerity and good faith: "The whole process of punishment is an ugly business at the best. The prisoners are unhappy, and are meant to be much less happy than others outside in this not too happy world. The conditions in jail must necessarily be squalid, the cost of maintenance narrowly scrutinized, since it is raised from the taxation drawn, in part, from the poorest of the poor; and the process of meting out measure for measure according to human standards must be crude, imperfect, and full of harsh discordances." He was, however, exploring the whole subject of prison administration. It is not too much to say that he had been led to this course in the first place by the campaign that Galsworthy had conducted, and secondly by *Justice*. In July he asked Galsworthy to visit him, and told him privately, as a few days later he would tell the House, that he was to put through a whole series of prison reforms which would include the reduction of solitary confinement to three months for recidivists and to one month for all other prisoners. He acknowledged in a final letter that "there can be no question that your admirable play bore a most important part in creating that atmosphere of sympathy and interest which is so noticeable upon this subject at the present time". (He neatly ducked the subject of pit ponies which Galsworthy had hopefully at the last moment raised.)

It is difficult to recall any play which could claim to have wielded comparable and specific influence of this kind. As Murray triumphantly wrote, "It is a fine thing to have achieved, a really great thing. Does not real life seem a tremendous thing as compared with art when one gets the two together?" He added, without perhaps his customary tact, "I mean, how much greater it is to have saved a lot of men and women from two months of solitary confinement than to have sent any number of over-fed audiences into raptures!"

XVII

By the year 1910 Galsworthy had thus become a figure in the land and a leader of the English theatre. In the following four years he wrote four major plays for the London stage—*The Pigeon, The Fugitive, The Mob* and *A Bit o' Love*—and saw his work widely produced through Europe and America. The plays were those of a successful playwright with nothing particularly new to say, but saying it efficiently. *The Fugitive* and *A Bit o' Love* both returned to Galsworthy's theme of a woman unhappy in marriage. In *The Pigeon*, in which Ferrand the tramp-philosopher was revived, a set of down-and-outs play on the sympathies of a man who cannot resist answering appeals for charity, no matter how aware he may be that he is being defrauded; and yet is noble by that very weakness. *The Mob*, written some years before the outbreak of war in 1914, was a curiously prophetic statement of the martyrdom of the genuinely conscientious objector, putting humanity above patriotism.

There is nothing in any of these plays to have established a great reputation but they kept his name securely before the public. So did his activity in public affairs. During the same years he became a recognized campaigner for humane causes and a noted initiator of correspondence in *The Times*; occasionally he felt so strongly that he accepted also the aid of the Northcliffe Press. His most ambitious and certainly least successful campaign was to persuade governments to agree to ban the use of the aeroplane as a weapon of war. He organized a letter of protest, to be signed by the eminent in science and the arts in many lands, though he met a few noteworthy rebuffs. Chesterton politely declined to put his name to an attempt to outlaw any special weapon. Arnold Bennett gently refused to sign anything so unpractical. Shaw told him outright that it was an absurdity and he knew perfectly well that aerial warfare would not be ruled out. "It may be horrible," he wrote, "but horror is the whole point of war; the newspapers will be really jolly when showers of shells alternate with showers of mangled aeronauts on crowded cities."

Galsworthy also advocated reform of the House of Lords, votes for women (though he deplored the violence of the Suffragettes) and, naturally, a revision of the divorce laws so as to allow an unhappy marriage to be dissolved without the hypocrisy of pretended sexual guilt. He jibbed, however, at putting his name to a demand for the abolition of capital punishment. His least publicized campaign was for help for the prostitutes of London, who had always moved him to a deep pity. His entirely unpublicized acts were those of private charity. Whether or not there was mixed in the motive a sense of guilt at his own good fortune, he was a genuinely charitable man, usually refusing to believe that he was being played upon by some unscrupulous beggar; he was a particularly "soft touch" for ex-convicts. No record remains of his private charities—save an occasional note of faint protest from Ada that he was being had. Marrot states, presumably on Ada's authority, that he made it a regular rule to live on less than half his income and to give the rest away.

The campaigns in which he was most absorbed were those to do with animals. He once told his nephew Rudo that while he wished to do what he could to ameliorate cruelty to both humans and animals, if it came to the choice he would choose the animals, since humans had at least some small capacity for aiding themselves. Besides the agitation about pit ponies, which Winston Churchill had adroitly side-stepped, Galsworthy was chiefly concerned with campaigns for the better and more humane regulation of slaughterhouses and for controlling or banning the use of animals as performers. He was also strongly opposed to zoos.

His only novel during the four years after 1910, *The Dark Flower*, was curiously different in its mood of sensual introspection from any of his earlier novels except only his very first most immature novel, *Jocelyn*, though it was to be followed by two others in something of the same mood, written during wartime, *Beyond* and *A Saint's Progress*. These three, but particularly *The Dark Flower*, were his breakaway from novels of social purpose. As he himself described it years later, "Disintegration set in; emotionalism streamed from me."

He was still writing about Ada and himself. But whereas in the earlier novels the circumstances of their life together had spurred him into an attack upon English society, in the *The Dark Flower* he turned inward and wrote emotionally of her as a woman. Although the novel relates the three passionate loves in the life of an artist, Mark Lennan—Spring, Summer and Autumn—Galsworthy began the writing with Summer, probably without any clear idea of the book as a whole or that this would be the middle of three episodes. Summer is the scarcely disguised passage of autobiography, already quoted, in which Lennan falls in love with an unhappily married woman, Olive Cramier, at Monte Carlo. It is Galsworthy's most clearly stated account of the beginnings of his love affair with Ada; accurate, if the death of Olive Cramier at the end of it, immediately after she has first given herself to Lennan, be accepted as a translation of a death wish.

When he had written that, it must have seemed to him incomplete unless it could be given its proper place in the development of his whole emotional life; he once included this novel in a list of those in which he felt he had best succeeded in setting down the truth as he believed it. So then he turned to Spring, in which a younger Lennan, as an undergraduate, falls passionately in love with the wife of his Oxford tutor, who herself relinquishes him in order that he may marry a childhood sweetheart, Sylvia. Apart from Sylvia, who must be a vague memory of Sybil Carr the singing teacher, there seems to have been no autobiography in the Spring section of the book. Autumn, in which the ageing Lennan is obsessed with an almost ludicrous passion for a young girl (and she for him), is one of the few oblique admissions Galsworthy makes that his marriage to Ada was not, after all, entirely the fulfilment of his sexual life; Soames Forsyte, as an old man, when he had largely become his author's mouthpiece, also discovers that a young girl can still stir the faun in him. There are hints of this, too, in the *Life and Letters*. Marrot, writing always to the instruction of the widowed Ada, has this: "He was widely regarded as an austere personality verging on the ascetic. Nothing could be further from the truth. Asceticism and a sense of beauty, though they may co-exist, can never harmonize; and Galsworthy's serene yet passionate love of beauty left no room for any jarring element. In truth he was a better, wiser, and more gifted man than is commonly found in a generation; for the rest, he was a man as others are. Only natural prudery, then, could have been capable of supposing that to his all-embracing love of beauty one form alone should prove elusive. He loved his wife as few men love theirs; that did not mean that he could feel the charm of no other woman. He realized, in fact—as many do not realize—that it is love rather than marriage that matters. If, when he was attracted to a woman, it amounted to nothing that mattered, it was not because he was married, but because he loved so profoundly the woman he had married. And if such a passing attraction was not destructive of self-respect in a singularly fastidious and self-respecting nature, we may conclude that Galsworthy was right in putting before the public (in *The Dark Flower*) in some need of instruction a point of view which it was reluctant or unable to discover for itself."

At the time it was published it was largely taken as an attack upon Christian standards of marriage as a whole. Even the devoted Gilbert Murray wrote to him uneasily, "You are thundering good as a Scriptor Eroticus, and it is a very good thing to be. But I rather wish you could treat in a novel the sort of broader theme you treat in your plays." From most critics it provoked censure, and to one such criticism, printed in the *Daily Mail*, Galsworthy made a fervid reply, though in private correspondence, not public column. The critic was Sir Arthur Quiller-Couch, who, having started by declaring, "I admire Mr Galsworthy greatly as an artist, and only on this side idolatry as a man telling necessary truths to this generation", nevertheless went on to condemn *The Dark Flower*, when stripped of its delicate writing, as something "pretty fatuous and sordid", and as putting forward as noble passion something almost indistinguishable from loose indulgence.

In the letter which he at once wrote to "Q", Galsworthy told him that he did not intend the novel to be anything but a study of Passion, "that blind force which sweeps upon us out of the dark and turns us pretty well as it will.... I did not think it an unworthy thing—nor indeed either quite fatuous or sordid—to try and paint Passion in terms of its spirit rather than as so many have painted it, in terms of the flesh; especially in a land whose Life and Art seem in a sort of perpetual conspiracy to blur and sentimentalize all the true values of the greatest force in life.... You use the word sentiment. [Quiller-Couch had in fact used the word "sentimentality".] Now, the longer I live the more constantly I notice that hatred of suffering, abhorrence of cruelty, is called sentiment only by those who have never fathomed, or truly envisaged the nature of that particular suffering or cruelty, and I am going to say quite frankly that though you are an older man than myself, of possibly wider general experience, you can never have looked first hand into the eyes of an unhappy marriage, of a marriage whose soul has gone or never was there, of a marriage that but lives on the meanest of all diet, the sense of property, and the sense of convention. You have never at first hand—as I have—seen souls shrivelling in bodies under that possibly worst form of suffering and worst kind of cruelty in the world. I am probably the most happily married man in England. I have seen at first-hand the two extremes. I know, as few of those—I would say as none of those—who glibly uphold marriage at all costs know, the value and beauty of a perfect union; and I know, as *certainly none* of them knows, the shrivelling hell of the opposite. And my gorge rises within me when I encounter that false glib view that the vow is everything, that people do better to go on living together (for nothing else *is* marriage) when one of them, or both, sicken at the other. A more fiendish spiritual destruction I would not wish any man than that he should continue to possess a woman who revolted at his touch; a more cruel existence for either man or woman I cannot imagine than that daily longing of their spirits when they try to live in comity, love not being there. I speak strongly, because I feel strongly, and know what I am talking about."

Of the sincerity of the letter and of Galsworthy's deep feelings there can be no doubt; but of its accuracy, as applied to Ada and himself, a doubt is permissible. In those passages about the despairs of the marriage where love is not, it is easy to recognize the somewhat brutal, overwhelming husband of the hapless Olive Cramier in the novel, but rather more difficult to see the retiring, reserved Major Arthur Galsworthy of real life, who for so many years had either not been "on terms" with Ada, or had been pursuing the affairs of the Essex Yeomanry at Colchester or of his country in South Africa. Galsworthy's letter to Quiller-Couch was of course about the Galsworthys, not the Cramiers. Moreover, if the facts of the past had thus been somewhat heightened in his memories of

159

it, could it be that the facts of the present—of his own marriage to Ada—had also been a little over-drawn? Possibly the word might be "sentimentalized"? Leaving aside all consideration of those passing attractions to other women that amounted to "nothing that mattered", could he really claim to be, at that time, probably the most happily married man in England?

A little earlier he had written of Ada, in a letter to Garnett, "I think of her sometimes as a piece of rare silk, with a bloom on it as delicate as that on grapes, but which you can't rub off, and spun of filaments, each one of which shines, but so subtly and so permanently blended that they can never come apart in colour or form. She is rare, but she is not rare with that obvious kind of rareness which jumps to the eye, and which consists in a person having certain qualities too strongly, and being called original. Her rareness is far more rare—it is the rareness and scent of the *fine fleur*, the perfect blend, no extreme in it, no violence. She has the grace and savour of the Cortina peasant women together with something in Reynolds's Countess of Albemarle (Nat. Gallery); both qualities are old. She goes back to nature in being as it were the last word in civilization. She is complex, but you cannot see the complexity because it is so beautifully put together. She is nymph-like in her soul, and, as you know, nymphs have an elusive permanence. All this is worse than Germanic—it is literary, it is also ill-expressed, perhaps inexpressible."

Such exaggerated lyricism in a letter to a friend in itself justifies the question as to whether he really knew or only persuaded himself into a fantasy that he knew, the value and beauty of a perfect union? If so, Ada's attitudes towards life seem inexplicable.

Everybody who knew John and Ada Galsworthy intimately (there are not many such) speaks of his quite extraordinary devotion to her. Viola Sauter, the niece who was to Ada almost as a daughter, says that she has never seen a man so wholly given over to a woman. He saw her always as the young woman in the portrait which Georg Sauter made of her in 1898, from which Galsworthy drew his image of Irene Forsyte. It is a portrait of a slightly built woman in a Worth dress, very upright; like her mother-in-law, Ada was never known to lounge back in a chair. The dress, something of a legend, was kept for long after, and Vi Sauter once tried, but failed, to get into it: it had a nineteen-inch waist. The impression of the portrait is of sensitive arrogance, aloofness (perhaps shyness). The eyebrows are unusually heavy, and, like the hair, very dark. But Galsworthy's retention of her in that image was a self-deception, for she did not remain like that. She became, not unnaturally with the pampering she received, self-centred, possessive and impatient of others. She always wanted to be in the right, says Vi Sauter, and she did not mind if she misused another person in order to put herself in the right. Galsworthy himself, describing his first heroine, Jocelyn, and therefore describing Ada as a young woman, wrote that she "loved generously to appreciate and to be appreciated, investing herself thereby with a great quality of attraction not lessened by the essential pride which forbade her to ask a favour from God or man. She never sought . . . to attract admiration or affection, yet without appreciation she drooped as a flower without water." From her earliest days with him, and until the end of his life, she was wrapped up in him and his writing to such a degree that she seemed almost to have merged her identity with his and certainly to have taken a large part in his work. But for all that and for all his devotion to her, she was plainly an unhappy woman and she grew unhappier and more neurotic with the years.

She was for ever setting up fences against the world, or running away from it by one means or another. Before they could marry, they had inevitably found their times of greatest hap-

161

piness together on journeys overseas, and at home had lived in a small, enclosed circle of a few old friends and a few members of the family. She never allowed him very much to enlarge it. Of the old friends, Conrad, Murray, Barrie, Masefield, a man named Frank Lucas and his wife, young Ralph Mottram (Ada's family friend and Galsworthy's protegé) and of course the Garnetts, just about made up the tally, which was not lengthened much beyond an agreeable but distant friendship with a French man of letters, André Chevrillon, and a warm acquaintance with Thomas Hardy. She strengthened the fences around this small group by her ever-increasing hypochondria, those recurrent lengthening bouts of rheumatism and asthma, those immense head-colds. The illnesses increased the ease with which she could keep herself away from life around her, and had the added advantage of providing Galsworthy with another, never-failing outlet for his devotion. He could nurse her. He did so with such inexhaustible patience and readiness that he discovered in himself an ability for nursing and—so he persuaded himself—a delight in it. He even found a derivation for it: he had inherited the taste from his mother. In fact, it was only nursing Ada that delighted him. In other people's ailments he took no pleasure and he could not bear to have contact with any sort of bodily deformity. This revulsion was so strong that it outweighed all his usual generous impulses. He once employed a gardener whose crippled wife was longing for some kindliness from him, but he had shamefacedly to admit that he could not bring himself to go near her.

Ada's other means of escape from the society in which Galsworthy had re-established her, and himself become a figure of respect, was to resume the wanderings abroad. During the first half-dozen years of their marriage they travelled little outside England. Those were the years of Galsworthy's most prolific and valuable writing, during which he established his reputation. They were also the years during which they devoted their affection to their spaniel, John (or Chris), the dog woven into the fabric of their love for each other. When Chris died just before the Christmas of 1911, their life too seemed ruptured. "Addison Road. Chris is gone," he noted in his diary for that day. "Ada prostrate. Oh! so sad a day!" He celebrated the dog in a sketch, "Memories", published the following year in a collection, *The Inn of Tranquillity*. For all his evident feeling for his dog, it is a formalized portrait expressing expected sentiments and falling far short of what a novelist of acute, hard intellect can make of the character of a dog; the sort of thing that can be found, for instance, perhaps best of all in Thomas Mann's *A Man and his Dog*.

About a year after the death of the dog, the Galsworthys moved out from Addison Road—the memories had become too painful, the place seemed dead without the spaniel—and took a flat in Adelphi Terrace. But before that, within a month of Chris's end, they were off on a journey abroad which was the first of a vast new series of travels. It was as though the death of the dog, the breaking of that link with her former, private years with Galsworthy, had released in Ada a yet stronger longing to get away from the world in which they were both well known and which had once so markedly shunned her. For it was she who insisted on the travels. She could settle nowhere. She had to be wandering continually from hotel to hotel, from country to country. He had no wish for such a peregrination but wanted simply to stay at home and get on with his writing. Since Ada wanted to travel, however, and he always granted even her whims, travel he must and perforce take his writing with him and do it on the way. Particularly he had to travel in the winter, when his idea of happiness was buttered toast in front of a wood fire in an English farmhouse with the wind howling comfortingly across Dartmoor outside; and a spaniel at his feet; and a J nib and bottle of ink handy. In winter, however, it became specially important to go abroad for the sake of Ada's health. Once he was abroad, he had to be dragged from his chair to go sightseeing. He was completely uninterested in being a tourist. The only places which stirred him were those which he had visited with Ada in the early days of their love. Otherwise he detested travelling, except by sea. But except for necessary crossings from one land to another, they never travelled by sea since Ada was a disastrously bad sailor. They went interminable train journeys and then long drives by car or carriage; in the evening, as like as not, Ada's asthma would come on more severely and he would sit in their hotel bedroom, heating glasses of milk for her and, to soothe her, reading out loud *Travels with a Donkey*. It became a family joke that this book lasted them for a quarter of a century as an asthma cure.

The tale of their travels at this time is long and varied. Once he had supervised the rehearsals of *The Pigeon* at the Royalty Theatre during January 1912, he and Ada set off for Paris and then on to the south of France, where they called upon the Arnold Bennetts. Scarcely were they back in London than on impulse they decided to visit the United States; the excuse was that they could see *The Pigeon* into production in New York. By now, too, Galsworthy's reputation as a novelist stood quite as high in America (where he was published by Scribner), as in his own country.

New York itself made the usual sort of impression on him; as he put in his notebook, "Blustery voyage, very cold towards the end, with bows sheathed in ice, into a clear bright New York. Strange town, strange juxtaposition of tall and short houses. Exhilarating air." While he was conducting the rehearsals of the play (with which, incidentally, Winthrop Ames's Little Theatre on 44th Street opened), Ada retired for a week's rest to Lakewood in New Jersey. Then they made a quick dashing tour through Boston, Chicago and out to the Grand Canyon, down which they rode for seven hours on mules. The usual tourist thing with the usual tourist reaction: "The most wonderful sight and masterpiece of Nature in the world, I think. Morning and afternoon, walking and gazing at the marvellous, mysterious, beautiful, rhythmic piece of shifting form and colour." They moved on towards San Francisco and, when they got to Santa Barbara, Galsworthy found that he could resume a full flow of writing even as he travelled; each morning he did his stint and then consented to sightseeing or to the modest lionizing. They skirted round through New Orleans, Washington ("touch of lumbago") and back to New York. In his notebook he started their curious habit of listing the people they had met, most of them never heard of, and he summed up his impressions of America thus, "Found curious state in America of aspiration towards good literature and art but practically no present production of it. Success still the standard, not the thing for the thing's sake. But success meaning perhaps less monetary success than it did. Terrible disposition to short cuts in everything, especially among dramatists. Drama in hands of commercial Jews mainly and no-one making resolute front against this. No central radiating point for art of any kind. New York trying but not succeeding. Therefore no standards. At the same time much apparent wish for change, to judge by talk. Found politics in most interesting state. Just hesitating on edge of chasm between the old Republican v. Democratic parties, now academic, dead; and new state of Capital v. Labour, hesitating to jump, but will jump. . . . In fact America very much at the mercy during this next generation of the chance outcrop of some men of genius, failing this in a bad way, spiritually. Lack of roots everywhere, more and more, instead of less and less, apparent. Curious phenomenon superficially but natural considering speeding up of communications and increased drifting tendency of population. New England traditions snowed under, Southern traditions mainly broken up, movement a whirl of everything everywhere, on top." He had, in short, found that America, for all the flattery with which it received him, was less English than he felt he had a right to expect. It was a great relief to find that they could make the return journey across the Atlantic in company, by good luck, of the Murrays. On the return voyage Ada, while feeling very seasick, set one of his poems to music. During the American journey indeed she had made songs out of several of his poems, the first collection of which, *Moods, Songs and Doggerels*, had been published in London while they were away. It was for long a sorrow to Galsworthy that his poetry was not treated with the respect that his plays and novels, or indeed his small literary essays, commanded. He privately considered it to be the finest of all his work but in truth very little of it amounts to more than competent versifying.

They were back from America in mid-May. By July they were travelling again, this time to Cortina, returning home via Austria, Germany and Belgium. All this time Galsworthy was working on *The Dark Flower* as well as revising the proofs of his collection of little essays and stories, *The Inn of Tranquillity*. They came back to Wingstone, he still busy at the novel; spent October in Manchester for a production of *The Pigeon*, November in London for the long-delayed play, *The Eldest Son*; and by December they were off once more to France, where they settled at Arcachon for the winter. The Chevrillons were there (so was d'Annunzio, "but though we saw him on his bicycle, followed by the bourgeois, we rather avoided making his acquaintance"). It took Ada some time to recover, in any event, from what Galsworthy noted as "the full enjoyment of horrible influenza". Here, in the intervals of nursing her and riding through the woods, he finished *The Dark Flower*, and then they took a trip to the Pyrenees.

After their return to England in the Spring of 1913, they had a short respite from travelling. Galsworthy was starting a new novel, *The Freelands*—the last sign of the weakened impulse to criticize contemporary society which had come originally from Ada's unhappiness. This was to be the novel in which he drew the portrait of his mother as Frances Freeland and he began by a visit to the districts around Malvern from which her family came and which he intended to use as his setting. It was in July of this year that they gave up the house in Kensington and moved into the top-floor flat at Adelphi Terrace. Hardly had they made the shift than Ada had to be away again. They set off, this time accompanied by his sister Lilian and her husband Georg, the painter, for Switzerland. They were home for the production of *The Fugitive* in September, first at the Court Theatre, then transferred to the Prince of Wales. Not much more than a fortnight later they left for Vienna, where *Justice* was being produced. They came back slowly, stopping at Wiesbaden for Galsworthy to have treatment for a shoulder he had damaged while riding in Devon during the summer. Once home again, they went at once to Yorkshire, Galsworthy to attend to a play production at Leeds and Ada to take a cure for her rheumatism. In December, when they were both "heavily water-logged with colds", they cleared off for Egypt. In the same ship they found Massingham, the journalist, and his wife, and joined with them into a party. It was a tourist trip, enlivened by lunch with Kitchener, to whom Massingham introduced them (Galsworthy found him "impressive but seeming rather to have lost edge"). They saw, of course, the Pyramids, the tombs of Luxor to which they travelled by train and Aswan to which they went by boat. After they had returned to Cairo they took a twelve-day journey into the desert with a dragoman and fifteen attendant Arabs. The desert delighted them both. They both felt unusually well (as most people do in the desert). Ada was enchanted with her camel, not having realized what a gentle companion a camel could be; on parting from it she could not resist kissing its "velvet nose". (Later she chanced to see two camels making love and was fascinated by the gentleness and lovingness of their movements.) Their Arabs were "a jolly lot, and interesting creatures, nice to us, at least". They were shown the usual tourist attractions of a desert trip. "Had a native dancer in the village of Fayoum, pretty creature, like a tiger cat," they wrote in their notebook. "Great fun that evening. Another evening our Arabs were dancing Dervishes, which was rather disgusting and alarming, on the Prophet's birthday. They also ate a ram whole, beak and bones."

All this time Galsworthy was writing. He had laid aside his novel for a time, and was engaged on the play, A Bit o' Love; he finished it in Sicily, to which they then journeyed, sitting in "a jolly hotel room with a jolly terrace attached, looking over to Etna, with almond-blossom in the foreground. Plenty of snow on Etna". They stayed there, indeed, for a fortnight during which Galsworthy finished his play, met Robert Hitchens, rambled round the hills, completed two short sketches and wrote a strong letter to The Times about delays in Parliament. At Viareggio on the way home they were both most disappointed by Shelley's grave—"Americanized". They were back in England in time for the first production of The Mob at the Gaiety Theatre, Manchester, at the end of March 1914. This was the play, once named The Patriot, about the idealist putting humanity above love for his country in time of war; it was transferred to a London theatre some three weeks later. Then they retired to Wingstone farm for Galsworthy to push ahead with his abandoned novel, The Freelands. His mother was by then living not far away in an hotel at Exmouth. As the summer came on, Ada developed a severe neuritis in the neck and took to her bed. By the end of July

Galsworthy was writing into his diary the sort of stupefied, bewildered protests common to all radicals at the sudden emergence of a threat of war: "These war-clouds are monstrous. If Europe is involved in an Austro-Servian quarrel one will cease to believe in anything. . . . Things going on working up for this awful catastrophe. I rode and walked with A. The suddenness of this horror is appalling. . . ." By August 1 Ada was attending a nursing-fund meeting and Galsworthy deciding to enquire about ambulance classes. On August 3, "A miserably anxious day, ourselves hovering on the verge of this war. . . . I hate and abhor war of all kinds; I despise and loathe it. And the thought of the million daily acts of its violence and hateful brutishness keeps riving my soul. I try not to think of all the poor creatures who are suffering and will suffer so terribly; but how not to? Wrote some words of Peace; but shan't send them anywhere. What's the use of whispering in a hurricane?" Then at last, on August 4, "The horror of the thing keeps coming over one in waves; and all happiness has gone out of life. I can't keep still, and I can't work. Ada manages to behave better, bless her. The temper of England seems finer than I thought it would be. There is little or no bluster, and much unity of resolution. If this war is not the death of Christianity, it will be odd. We need a creed that really applies humanism to life instead of talking of it. God in the mouths of all these potentates—the word does not beseem them. A meeting of the Rifle Club Committee."

XVIII

On the second day of the war a constable called at Wingstone farm and told Galsworthy that his mare, Peggy, must be taken into Moretonhampstead on the morrow to the horse muster. To Galsworthy this was an extra blow of particular cruelty. "Poor thing," he wrote in his diary. "But they can hardly take a mare who was lame a week ago, and still has an open wound, to say nothing of her desperate illness last year." He went anxiously into Moretonhampstead next day but to his great relief Peggy was rejected for active service: "I am thankful. The poor dear wouldn't have stood rough work for a week. She seemed to know that something was up, and to be relieved as I rode her home."

It was not long before he was considering his own position. His thoughts on the war which he contributed to Scribner's magazine under that title were at first a jumble of horror, of indignation at the fatuity of it and pity at the additional suffering it would cause to those millions of people on both sides who were on the verge of want at the best of times; on August 6 he had written to *The Times*, urging the setting-up of a War Relief Fund for that kind of necessity. Money, of course, he could give and freely gave. By early in November he had noted in his diary that his contribution to various war funds came to £1,250 so far: "I.e. Motor Ambulance £400. Belgian relief £300. Cigarettes £250. Prince of Wales £200. Authors and Actors £100. Small Funds £50. M.E.R. £50. Devon £50. Queen's Women's £25. Belgian Refugees £25." (The agitation of the moment no doubt accounted for the faulty arithmetic.) "Very early we sent off all sadlery and horsecloths we could spare," wrote Ada, "Zeiss field glasses, a motor ambulance to France, a motor launch and later one (the *John and Ada*) to Gallipoli." Galsworthy's peacetime rule that more than half of his income should be given away to those in need seemed now insufficient. Throughout the war he gave away, Marrot estimates, probably three-quarters of it, including all his literary earnings; though Ada, writing after his death, says it was his literary earnings in America that were so disposed. Either way it was a considerable sum, and the thought that this, at least, he could contribute to his country was the spur he needed to start him writing again. He quickly finished off the novel, *The Freelands*, which he had been working at for more than a year and had twice laid aside. This was the pendant to the four "class" novels, in which his satirical impulse faded out; it marked the end of the turmoil stirred in his life by his love for Ada, the stealth and secrecy of their ten years of waiting and the ignominy and anger of the divorce. It is the book which contains the portrait of his mother as Frances Freeland, written when she was living in failing health not far away at Exmouth, and revised as she lay in her last illness at Torquay where she was settled into rooms with her own servant. It contains, too, an uneasily questioning portrait of himself, the radical writer, assured of the validity of his advanced views and yet seeing disaster engulf his family without having the smallest notion of how to remedy it. The novel was a failure when it was published. The tyranny of the squirearchy over the lives of farm labourers was no longer an issue when the labourers had gone off with the squires' sons to Flanders. Galsworthy knew this, of course, and would most probably have abandoned the novel incomplete, had it not been for his desire to "make money for the country". In this it succeeded very well. When he finished the rough draft on October 1, 1914, he wrote in his diary, "It has been a pull to concentrate on it since the war began, but I have earned

£1,500 for the serial rights in Scribners, and this was the most substantial thing I could do for the relief funds."

He was writing at this time too a number of short essays and articles on war subjects. As Ada put it, he became "the Appeal writer *par excellence*; for refugees, for camp libraries, for vegetables for the Fleet, for cigarettes to soldiers, for London horses to be better fed, for Belgians to have a good Christmas dinner, for the Fund for Nurses, for the Children's Jewel Fund, for many another good cause, and for every gift book that appeared, to the best of my memory, something was written by him". He had attended a meeting in London of literary men "to concert measures of putting forward principles for which England is fighting". He had taken a Belgian refugee painter and his family into his care. But still, nagging ever at his mind, was the question of what part he personally and physically ought to play in the war effort. He was already forty-seven years of age, so there was no real question of his volunteering for the Army; though he was perhaps uneasily aware that Major Arthur Galsworthy, who was seven years older, married again and the father of an infant son, had at once wangled himself a commission in the Somersets, was training at Andover and was later to serve for a time in France. Galsworthy could not reasonably have been expected, however, to model his conduct on that of Ada's first husband, whose lifelong infatuation with all things military (and probable boredom with his modest, idle country life) had led him to active service at the age of fifty-four. It did not seem to Galsworthy then, or at any time during the war, that he was called upon to take personal part in the fighting. His crisis of conscience came from an agonized speculation as to whether or not he would have volunteered, had he been of military age. Reluctantly and in shame he told himself that the answer was probably that he would not. "The heart searchings of this War are terrible," he wrote in his diary in November 1914, "the illumination of oneself rather horrible. I think and think what is my duty, and all the time know that if I arrived at certain conclusions I shouldn't do that duty. This is what comes of giving yourself to a woman body and soul. A. paralyses and has always paralysed me. I have never been able to face the idea of being cut off from her.

"In cool blood I suppose what I am doing—that is writing on—novels and stories—and devoting all I can make, especially from America—no mean sum—to Relief—is being of more use than attempting to mismanage Relief Funds, or stretcher-bearing at some hospital, or even than training my elderly unfit body in some elderly Corps.

"I say to myself, 'If I were young and unmarried I should certainly have gone! There is no doubt about that!' But there is great doubt whether if I had been of military age *and married to A.* I should have gone. Luckily for my conscience I really believe my game shoulder [the one he had injured while riding a few years earlier] would not stand a week's training without getting my arm in a sling. Moreover I suppose there is no one as yet training as short-sighted as I am. Still I worry—worry—all the time—bald and grey and forty-seven and worrying. Funny!"

To absolve himself a little he plunged into work on another novel, *Beyond*, to earn money "for the country". He began it at the very end of 1914 on a Christmas visit to his mother at Torquay and plodded away at it throughout the following year, mostly at Wingstone, where Ada developed an attack of influenza which lasted her from February until June, off and on. This was his main task, though he undertook any smaller request that was made to him—a sketch for an album on behalf of blinded soldiers, an appeal for Belgian Relief, more Thoughts on the war, an earnest plea on behalf of the R.S.P.C.A. for funds to alleviate the suffering of horses at the Front. He also, much to his distress, went out to shoot rabbits at Wingstone—the first living things he had shot for fourteen years. He did it to save the rabbits from being trapped, which he regarded as the even greater evil. Moreover, the thought of his "elderly, unfit body", while comforting as a reason for inaction, in itself distressed him. He began, therefore, each morning on rising, to perform the set of physical exercises advocated in an admirable little book in a bright yellow cover by a Swede named Mueller, which were at that period something the fashion. A regular attention to Mueller toned him up nicely, and reduced his weight to 12 stone 1 pound. "I no longer fear obesity," he confided to a friend.

His mother died in May, with himself and Lilian at her bedside. All the family except Ada (who was too ill with her influenza) attended the funeral at Highgate, where his mother was buried in his father's grave. His comments in his diary were saddened but unemotional: "Dear soul! The long sleep be good to her! ... A brave soul at rest."

Early in 1916 he finished *Beyond*, an indifferent novel about a woman named Gyp (modelled a good deal on Ada) and her unhappy marriage to a Swedish violinist. Galsworthy himself declared this long novel to be his worst-written; he had pressed ahead with it in order to gain, for the Relief Funds, the value of serial rights in an American magazine.

At about this time the war struck into the heart of his own family. Georg Sauter was interned. His young son, Rudo, who had been studying in Munich until just before the war began, was restricted to a five-mile radius of their home at Holland Park Avenue. Galsworthy was deeply distressed and angered at the fatuity of it. What could be more stupid than to intern an ageing artist who had spent most of his adult life in England, was married to an Englishwoman and was, save for the actual fact of naturalization, virtually English himself? The additional restrictions on the freedom of his own nephew, Rudo, to whom he and Ada were devoted—and, indeed, of his own sister, Lilian—appalled him. He at once wrote a Petition for Sauter's release, sending it with a personal letter to the Home Secretary. He himself went to the Home Office and put the case to Herbert Samuel, who could do nothing but refer it back to the tribunal dealing with internees. In May, Galsworthy appealed in person to an Advisory Committee in Westminster Hall, but without avail. All he could do was to get police permission for Lilian and Rudo to travel down to Wingstone, for anti-German feeling was running so high in London that he feared the consequences of their German name. He also got permission to see Sauter himself for an hour in his internment camp at Wakefield. He found him bitter and angry, and travelled back from Leeds to Devon, scarcely knowing what to report to his sister. For Lilian, of course, was in the deepest distress. She perceived that her life had been smashed, as indeed it had. When, at a later period of the war, Georg Sauter was released from internment under an arrangement for the exchange of elderly and sick internees, he went back to Germany, cursing England and all things English. On his arrival at Berlin he made a series of somewhat notable portraits of German military commanders. He would have nothing more to do with England (save that, in his old age, when he married for a second time, he again married an Englishwoman). Lilian did not feel, either while the war was still in progress or when it was ended, that she could live in Germany. The Sauters' marriage was therefore in effect ended by Georg's internment; the son remained with his mother in England and was more and more regarded by Galsworthy and Ada as their responsibility, almost as if he had been their own son.

Meanwhile Galsworthy had at last found the salve for his conscience, the physical act of duty which he could bring himself to perform. He had offered, on behalf of the whole family, the house at 8 Cambridge Gate as a hospital; it was later used, in fact, as a wounded soldiers' club, and Galsworthy had it fitted for this purpose at his own expense. When in September 1916 he went to Red Cross Headquarters to discuss this, he met by chance on the steps of that building an old friend, Dorothy Allhusen, who was busily engaged in wartime hospital work. She suggested that he and Ada should go out to a small French military hospital with which she was concerned at Die, near Valence, where rheumatic and neurasthenic French soldiers were being treated. Galsworthy could massage the patients and Ada could look after the store of linen. He seized upon the idea with alacrity. The impossibility of leaving Ada had hitherto prevented him from going to the war; here was an opportunity for him and Ada to go to the war together. He at once set about taking a course of lessons in Swedish massage and Ada delightedly designed a becoming nurse's uniform for herself, which the authorities would not permit her to wear. Galsworthy trained at massage for a month, assiduously practising at home on Ada. In mid-November they both put on khaki and crossed the Channel. "Great sense of exhilaration," he noted, "at getting out of England."

After a couple of days in Paris, during which they could lunch with the Chevrillons, dine at Garnier's and meet Ralph Mottram who happened to be there after a spell of service in the trenches, they took train to Die and began work at the little hospital where Mrs Allhusen and three other English-women formed the staff caring for thirty-five patients. Ada sat most of the day sewing at the linen. Galsworthy massaged some eight to ten soldiers each day, writing home to his sister Mabel that "oddly enough" his massage seemed to be of some use. To perform this task was more difficult for him than it would have been for most men. He had not lost his horror of any kind of disease or deformity of body and it was only by an incessant effort of will that he forced himself to physical contact with such. Every afternoon the half hour before tea must have been a most welcome diversion for him; in that half hour he led the patients through the pattern of exercises he had acquired from the excellent Mueller to control his own threatened obesity.

In his notebook he jotted, "Friendly people, hardish work and cold weather. . . . Beautiful country, mountains, Lombardy poplars, rivers, cypresses, wood-smoke, Roman remains, friendly people. A very cold winter, sometimes 20 to 30 degrees of frost, Fahrenheit. A little black dog, whom we called Aristide, came and made his home in our little apartment. A tapestried bedroom, big wood fire, a sort of monks' cell for dining-room, a broad veranda the other side, a little garden of bare plane trees just below. The proprietress of the chateau lived in the same house, Madame Benoit, with her companion, Mlle de Lucy; they were very affable. We never got so near the French people before. The *poilus* were wonderfully nice; grateful and on the whole open about themselves, much more so than our Tommies. Two tragic cases." (They were cases of mental distress, of which he wrote a sketch published later in a collection, *Tatterdemalion*; the hospital yielded him material for three somewhat moving sketches.)

By March their tour of duty was ended. When they drove away, the little black papillon dog, Aristide, broke loose and went running hopelessly after them. Since they were already in France, they took the opportunity to have a fortnight's holiday, mostly at a little inn just outside Marseilles, where Ada could recover from a bruised shin sustained in a fall at the hospital and Galsworthy give his sciatica a chance to get better. Then they had a week in Paris, seeing everybody. On March 28 they landed back in London, content that they had done their bit, but quite exhausted; Ada went down at once with 'flu, followed not long after by a bad bout of rheumatism, which meant a journey to Clifton for radiant-heat treatment. While they were there, Galsworthy tortured himself by a visit to the zoo, about which he wrote a protesting poem, "Pitiful".

XIX

They spent the rest of the war in England, mostly at Wingstone. Lilian and Rudo were in a nearby cottage and Mabel came with her husband and children to take a bungalow in the district. Galsworthy and Ada made occasional journeys to London, sometimes sharing the Adelphi Terrace basement with Barrie during air raids. They took holidays chiefly at Littlehampton, a small seaside town to which they had long been partial. His play, *Foundations*, was produced in London and failed quickly. "It has become quite clear that I can never hope for a financial success with a play in London," he wrote, with a touch of irritability, to his sister Mabel. "It's an unspeakable public. I think I must certainly hold the dramatic record for all countries—eleven plays produced, and not one (*in London*) has made a penny for the management that produced it. When you think of it this is a remarkable feather in one's cap. I've taken managers in eleven times, though they all know perfectly well that all my plays are financial failures, or at all events, don't make money."

Towards the end of 1917 the customary restlessness came upon Ada and, since they could not travel abroad, they travelled at home. They journeyed to Monmouthshire, spent a time with the Masefields at Oxford, took a brief walking tour in Sussex (where they were thinking of buying a country house), made a trip to Lancashire for the production of a play, wandered back again into Sussex and then came up to London where they started negotiations to buy a town house, Grove Lodge, in Hampstead. Ada was in and out of bed at this time with "that 'flue", so he took her down to the Beach Hotel at Littlehampton for Christmas.

179

After dinner on December 31 they were in their sitting-room at the hotel with two friends when Galsworthy was handed a telegram from the Prime Minister, "Please wire by return whether you accept offer of knighthood."

He was badly upset, having long felt that "between Letters and such honours there is and should be no such liaison". So he at once wired back to Lloyd George, "Most profoundly grateful but feel I must not accept."

As he and Ada went to bed, he remarked that he feared they might be too late, as indeed they were. The list of New Year Honours had already been sent to the newspapers, all of which therefore, on the following morning, published the announcement of a knighthood for John Galsworthy. He was in great distress and wired again to the Prime Minister, insisting that the honour should be cancelled: "Wired you on receiving your telegram last night that I could not accept knighthood I see it announced this morning am most sorry acceptance would be contrary to all my feeling and conviction must therefore persist in refusal and await your kind correction in the Press." That dispatched, he at once sat down to write to him, explaining that "I am indeed grieved to appear churlish towards so kind a thought, or priggish for refusing what is given to, and accepted by, much better men. But I have long held and expressed the conviction that men who strive to be artists in Letters, especially those who attempt criticism of life and philosophy, should not accept titles. I cannot smother down this feeling, or, believe me, I would have, sooner than cause you the inconvenience of annulling the announcement. I am hoping to see the laurels removed by correction in the Press at the earliest opportunity, for I feel in a remarkably foolish position at the moment."

The contradiction duly went forth that day (the explanation was that an earlier letter containing the offer of the knighthood must have gone astray). The newspapers, of course, telephoned to inquire from Galsworthy what had occurred. "By a stroke of good luck," he wrote in his diary, "I say Literature is its own reward." The story of the knighthood refused received even more prominence, naturally, than the earlier announcement of it. Letters and telegrams poured in. It remained for Thomas Hardy, with whom the Galsworthys now had a firm acquaintance, to write, rather spitefully, "I don't think that mistake about the knighthood a disaster for you exactly, and probably you don't by this time. A friend of mine who happened to be here said 'He has scored both ways. He has had the honour of being knighted, and the honour of having refused a knighthood. Many men would envy him.' I said I would tell you this."

The comment was unjust, for in such a matter Galsworthy was incapable of an ulterior motive; in things touching the dignity of his Art, he was humourlessly sincere.

Shortly after, his nephew, Rudo Sauter, was interned. He was staying at Manaton with his mother and with Viola Brookman, the girl whom he was later to marry, who was then acting as companion to Mrs Sauter. The local policeman, who had known Rudo since childhood, arrived in a state of embarrassment to arrest him. Lilian insisted on going to London with him and Vi accompanied her. Galsworthy, deeply depressed, exerted all the influence he could to have Rudo released but succeeded only in preventing his being sent to the internment camps in the Isle of Man.

Throughout all this he was just finishing his last complete novel written during the war, about a girl whose soldier lover is killed before he can marry her, but after their baby has been conceived. Even in wartime Galsworthy would scarcely have troubled with this familiar theme alone. For him, A Saint's Progress was worth writing because of the character of the girl's father, a clergyman, a good man in himself but so narrow-mindedly concerned with the conventions of morality of his church that his very insistence on goodness mars and nearly destroys his daughter's life. In this long exposition of his pitying scorn for organized religion and in the careful and truthfully-drawn setting of wartime life in England lies what value there is in the novel. It was not well received, and although Barrie told him that it was a fine book and Mrs Hardy wrote to say that she was reading it aloud, every word, to her husband, and thought that he preferred it to any other of Galsworthy's books, he himself did not think much of it.

What he had been writing to much better effect, at odd times during the war but mostly in 1916, were five long-short stories which he put together under the title *Five Tales*. The collection was published in July 1918, a tremendous month for him. During its early days, when the Great War was patently coming to an end, he was summoned to appear before a Medical Board to be examined for his fitness for military service. At the time he was not far short of his fifty-first birthday. He went before the Board at Exeter on July 15, and was rejected as permanently and totally unfit for military service and discharged from all liability for it. He dismissed the incident with a short note in his diary, but it seemed nevertheless to have a curiously liberating effect upon him as though, from that day onwards, he could feel that the duty about which he had fretted so conscientiously in 1914 had now officially been completed. It was as though the war, which had enmeshed him in misery and sapped his creative powers, was on that day ended for him and he could turn his thoughts ahead.

Chiming with this was the publication on July 25 of *Five Tales*. One of them, "The Indian Summer of a Forsyte", was an epilogue to *The Man of Property*. It was in this appendix that he retreated from the bitter ending of the novel (to which Edward Garnett had so strongly objected), with Irene returning, beaten and desolate to her life with Soames now that her lover, Bosinney, was dead. Galsworthy had intended without any doubt that Irene was doomed for the rest of her life to live with the man she loathed. That was to be the tragic ending of his novel and the justification of his attack on property —the emptiness of its victory.

But in the epilogue it is declared that, on the contrary, Irene had left Soames on the very same night of her return to his house and left him for good. Now it is more than three years later. Old Jolyon has bought Robin Hill from Soames— the house that Soames had built for Irene, and was never to live in. Irene has wandered back to it and old Jolyon, stumbling across her, has come to know her, almost to love her for her beauty and pathos. It is when she is coming to Robin Hill that old Jolyon gently dies, on a summer's day, seated under the oak tree before the house, with the old dog Balthasar stretched on the lawn by his side.

Galsworthy himself wrote, "Towards the end of the war came the volume called *Five Tales*, and restored me to my pigeonhole. It did more than that, for it started again within me love, or—shall I say—interest in the Forsytes."

But this self-judgment is quite at fault. "The Indian Summer of a Forsyte", to which he is of course referring, did not in the least restore him to his pigeonhole. On the contrary, it made him a quite different novelist from the man who wrote *The Man of Property*, and completely changed his whole Forsyte theme. The epilogue took all the edge off *The Man of Property*, blunted its satire, polished it into kindliness and humanity. It could not furnish Irene with the happy ending that Garnett had suggested—she and Bosinney going off together to Paris, joyful and unafraid. But it deprived the novel of the bitterness with which Galsworthy had written it, some fifteen years earlier, in the midst of his personal turmoil over Ada's divorce. He betrayed his own purpose but he made the Forsyte idea much more acceptable to the English reader. Mrs Thomas Hardy wrote that she had found it a joy to read *Five Tales* aloud to her husband. ("Read it very carefully and slowly," he had bade her, "because it's Galsworthy.") When she had read "The Indian Summer of a Forsyte", she felt that she could in future read *The Man of Property* "without a feeling of terrible despair". This is what, in truth, he had done with his epilogue. But it was by no means all that he had done. Having thus made *The Man of Property* acceptable to the ordinary reader, he had turned it into a possible prologue for a whole long history of the Forsytes, the people whom he basically wished to write about, because they were the people to whom he naturally, and now in sympathy, belonged.

It took him three days after the publication of *Five Tales* to grasp this. Sitting in the sunshine at Wingstone, he suddenly received the inspiration which was to govern almost the whole of the rest of his life.

"The idea of making *The Man of Property* the first volume of a trilogy," he noted, "cemented by 'The Indian Summer of a Forsyte' and another short episode, came to me on Sunday, July 28th, and I started the same day. This idea, if I can ever bring it to fruition, will make *The Forsyte Saga* a volume of half a million words nearly; and the most sustained and considerable piece of fiction of our generation at least. . . . But shall I ever bring it off?"

It is evident that, on that July Sunday at Wingstone, which he once described to Granville-Barker as the happiest day of his writing life, he had conceived at any rate the first and major part of his grand Forsyte design. What he had not perceived was that he could complete that design only by frustrating his original purpose for ever; or, if he did perceive it, it is doubtful whether he even understood his own underlying motive. Now that he had brought Ada back into respectability, back into the Forsyte family, and the intervening war had erased all public memories of his early personal scandal, it was necessary for the original novel of protest to be hidden by the huge humanity—sometimes even sentimentality—of the saga of English prosperous family life.

XX

Although he was already in his fifties, the end of the war seemed to release in Galsworthy such a stream of energy and joy that he in effect began a new career rather than continued his old one. Hitherto he had been a novelist and playwright of distinction, no more, still a little tainted with Bohemianism and the half-forgotten scandal of his earlier life. Now he was preparing to become a man of letters of international acclaim. He had long expunged from his mind the rebellious thoughts of his first years of writing, retaining only a gently humane, liberal attitude towards the brashness and freedom of the postwar years, which he regarded with a quiet disapproval worthy of any clubman; it would not be long before he was accepted into the Athenaeum. There were a few vestiges of his wartime activities—a skit in the form of a novel written pseudonymously, and a magazine, *Reveille*, which he had undertaken to edit for a government department on behalf of disabled soldiers—but he soon divested himself of these. He had in his mind now the scheme for the trilogy that, if he could pull it off, would place him at the head of contemporary English writing, in the staunchest sense of the word "English". A few days before the Armistice he had already moved from the little flat in the Adelphi to the imposing Hampstead house, Grove Lodge. A few days after the Armistice he expressed his happiness by going to Ware in Hertfordshire and buying a pedigreed Dandie Dinmont pup named Robin, which was to become the second most dear dog to him and Ada in their lives. For them, dogs were always the symbols of happiness or distress. The first and dearest was the black spaniel, John, or Chris, or any one of three score endearing nicknames, which they got while they were still engaged in their clandestine love affair and which lasted them throughout the first few, happiest years of their married life. This spaniel was of such significance to both of them, but particularly to Ada, that she records that when it died, "I was for some hours dangerously ill". Shortly afterwards, she declared, it returned to her as an apparition. She and Galsworthy were seated at dinner with one guest in their Addison Road house when she saw the spaniel enter the room, walk under the table, come out and gaze at the chair in which Galsworthy usually sat (though that evening the guest occupied it) and then simply disappear. "It is the only apparition I have ever seen," she wrote, in a book she published after Galsworthy's death, "for I am by no means psychic." She did not mention the apparition at the time and it is not clear whether she ever discussed it with her husband.

After the spaniel's death they both felt for some years that they could not contemplate having another dog, though there were farm dogs around them at Wingstone. Canine affection returned to their lives with the little black papillon, Aristide, which adopted them at the hospital in France during the war —at the time when they were suddenly happier again, since they were doing their bit. When they got back to England they cared for a few strays on Dartmoor—dogs were being turned off the farms because of dearth of food. One of these, indeed, a sheepdog bitch named Biz, they themselves bought when there was some risk of its being discarded, since it was no good at herding sheep, and at Hampstead, as the war ended, they were happy for a time with one of Biz's puppies. Robin, the Dandie Dinmont, the first to be bought of deliberate design since the death of the original black spaniel, symbolized the access of joy and the sense of new life which Galsworthy felt directly the Armistice was signed. As the years grew ever more successful, the number of dogs they purchased increased

—two red setters, a huge Alsatian, two more spaniels, a Dalmatian which suffered from hysteria, a Scottie, a bobtail and a Bedlington. Some were kept in country, some in town. But never again, except when he travelled abroad from England, was Galsworthy to lack a dog or two at his horse's feet, or lying by the side of his chair while he wrote his morning's stint; and never again was he to want recognition, fame, increasing wealth and honours, a happiness bred sedately from contentment, love of his fellow creatures, a public aloofness from them, and a private life confined within a small circle of family and a few friends.

Whether Ada shared this growing contentment with life is, however, doubtful. She never indicated by written or spoken word that all was not serene, but her neuroticism steadily deepened, her psychosomatic illnesses further increased. A simple cold in the head could now contrive to put her into bed for weeks, usually at what ought to have been times of special interest and pleasure for them both. An attack of "flue" endured sometimes for months. To her rheumatism she added neuritis and sciatica and when those failed her, asthma came on with enhanced severity. She continued, also, to lead Galsworthy on those restless overseas journeys, every winter and often during the summer, during which he spent the mornings, with blotter on knee, J nib and bottle of ink, composing the novels and plays which were to assure his fame; and the afternoons and evenings, as often as not, tending an invalid Ada in an hotel bedroom, heating glasses of milk, administering hot-water bottles and equably reading aloud from *Travels with a Donkey*, *The Pickwick Papers* or the chapter of the Forsyte chronicle which he had written that day. It was as if she still felt the compulsion to flee the society that had once ostracized her, even though it would now, given the opportunity, lionize her husband and accept herself. At this time, too, she was still trying to keep a youthful appearance;

when her hair began to turn, she dyed it and would not for many years let it show naturally white.

The first postwar journey was not, in fact, dictated by Ada, who would probably have preferred a winter in southern Europe, but by an invitation to Galsworthy to represent English literature at the Lowell Centenary dinner in New York. So to America in February 1919 they duly went. The ship was full of Canadian troops returning home, and was very cold "because they were trying to blow the influenza out of her". Ada, who had a fierce head-cold, nursed it in her cabin throughout the voyage and for the first nine days in her hotel bedroom in New York, leaving to Galsworthy all the interviews, the publicity and the rushing, through which Scribners guided him as carefully as possible. After the dinner and a stay in New England for Galsworthy to deliver some university lectures, they broke for sunshine and a holiday in the Carolinas, tasted plantation life, and ventured into the deep South. Then it was a combination of holiday and lecturing, right up through the Middle West, past Niagara (which they considered "very imposing, but unloveable") and home through New York. Galsworthy found the lecturing, as always, most fatiguing. He took immense pains to prepare a lecture, regarded it as a most serious enterprise and performed it well, drawing surprising strength from what was normally a quiet voice. But he did this only at the cost of severe nervous strain. He ended each lecture in such a lather of sweat that he had to be taken away and given a bath. To a man of reserve and diffidence it was torture to stand before a thousand students and speak for an hour. He did it out of a sense of duty: it was expected of a man of letters of his eminence. Most of the proceeds of lecturing went to charities.

In addition to the lecturing and the travelling, he was now engaged on his most important piece of sustained novel-writing, *The Forsyte Saga*. Throughout the American journey he worked steadily at *In Chancery*, the second novel of the trilogy. By the time he and Ada returned to England in May 1919 he had a substantial part of it drafted. They went to Wingstone at the end of May in fine weather and there the novel went well. He knew as he wrote it that his conception of the grand trilogy was being fulfilled, that he could in fact pull off this feat—that he had the power which, at the first moment, he had hesitantly doubted. Indeed, in his energy and exuberance in this immediate postwar time, he broke away from the novel after another month, and, in less than three weeks, wrote a play, *The Skin Game*. He wrote it "straight on end", first at Wingstone, then at Hampstead, revising it during a quick tour of Ireland, a visit to the Masefields and a subsequent few days in Scotland. When it was produced in the spring of the following year, it was at once his first commercial success in the London theatre. This was the first play he had written from his postwar attitude of mind. It had no particular social purpose nor did it make any propaganda point. It was simply a dramatic tale of conflict between the squirearchy and the new-rich, between old-style country life and new-style industrial power. When, later, it was produced in the United States, it was equally successful and for the same reason. It was the work of a skilled, experienced playwright whose rebellion had ended, who accepted without further struggle the society which had already accepted him and who therefore no longer had anything of much importance to say. As a corollary, of course, he no longer required the audience to do anything except enjoy itself. It re-established him as a leading dramatist.

Thus encouraged, he regularly broke away from the long trilogy of novels to write more plays. The first two, *A Family Man* and *Windows*, were not much of a success. The former, the story of a provincial tycoon who destroys his own small world through self-importance, was written to the correct formula for success, but somehow just missed the accomplishment; the latter, which returned to a theme of social justice —the rejection by the respectable world of a girl who has served a sentence for infanticide—and which was added to a cycle of Galsworthy plays produced at the Royal Court Theatre by Leon M. Lion, was too much in Galsworthy's old manner to be acceptable from the author of *The Skin Game*. The London audience now demanded only that kind of play from him and in March 1922, with the production of *Loyalties* at the St Martin's Theatre, they got it. When Galsworthy finished writing this play about a young officer, distinguished during the war, who in peacetime commits a crime (and pays the inevitable price of suicide), he remarked to Ada, "No Manager will refuse this." He knew very well, as the critics also knew, that this was only what the *Daily Chronicle* called "a closely-packed drama of adventure, a crook drama written by a master hand". But he was never again to have such a success in the theatre, except for *Escape*, which was in a sense similarly a crook drama on the chase theme, written by the same master hand.

These plays would in themselves have been a sufficient task for many a writer. From *The Skin Game* to *Escape*, he wrote and presented to the public seven plays in less than six years; three of them were the outstanding theatrical successes of their time. But for Galsworthy, in his exuberant postwar period, play-writing was little more than a relaxation from his chief task, things to dash off in a few weeks and upon which to expend only a few more weeks of intensive rehearsal. His true writing life was enmeshed now with the Forsytes. "From 1918 to the death of Soames, when the Forsyte Chronicles came to an end," he himself wrote, "I lived in and with that family." Completing the first half of the *Chronicles*, *The Forsyte Saga*—in itself the whole scheme that he had conceived on that afternoon at Wingstone in the summer of 1918

—took him little more than two years. He wrote *In Chancery*, as has been seen, steadily throughout his crowded American journey, and continued it during the summer of 1919, spent mostly at Wingstone but partly in Scotland and Ireland. Although he had broken off from the narrative to write *The Skin Game*, he finished the novel by November. He had then, as he confided in a letter to André Chevrillon, to write one further linking story and a third novel to make the whole *Forsyte Saga*.

XXI

In Chancery is the novel that shaped the whole future of the *Forsyte Chronicles* by setting Soames Forsyte firmly into the position of central character. The linking short story, "The Indian Summer of a Forsyte", giving *The Man of Property* the "happy" ending which the author when young had never intended for it, had made the rest of the *Saga* possible. *In Chancery* set its course. It brings the family story forward to the last year of the old century and runs it into the early years of the new. Soames, after seven lonely years at Brighton after his wife Irene had left him, has bought a riverside house at Mapledurham near Reading, in which to hang the pictures he is collecting; and with the house comes the old desire for a family, a son to whom he can leave his property. He is attracted to Annette, the daughter of a Frenchwoman who runs a restaurant in Soho, but his old longing for Irene has never left him. Why should they not, after so many years, become man and wife again? It is only when Irene turns from him with horror and flees to Paris that, in indeterminate misery, he puts the most private of private detective agencies to watch her. He wants a son, so he must suffer the acute and public agony of a divorce.

After an excellent piece of comedy in which the detective agency triumphantly reports the visit to Irene in Paris of a strange man who is in fact Soames himself, he gets his divorce because Irene and young Jolyon are falling in love. Young Jolyon is now a noted water-colour artist and lives at Robin Hill, the house which Soames originally built for Irene and which old Jolyon bought from him after the disaster of his marriage. It is to Robin Hill that Soames, choking with memories, goes to ask Irene for the last time to return to him and tells her he will withdraw the writs for divorce. He meets merely the contemptuous cry from her, "Guilty". What was not true before shall become so. She and young Jolyon do not contest the divorce action, but simply go away together to Italy (as Galsworthy had gone with Ada) while it takes its course.

Around this central theme Galsworthy built also the rest of the family history. Soames's sister, Winifred, has been deserted by her husband, Montague Dartie who, to the sick dismay of their son Val—just going up to Oxford—has run off to South America with a dancer. It is Soames's efforts to get Winifred a divorce in time that brings Monty back, broken but still a rogue, to be welcomed by Winifred despite all his faults. Val Dartie, meanwhile, has fallen in love with Holly, young Jolyon's daughter by his second, earlier marriage; he and her brother Jolly go off to the Boer War together in the Yeomanry; Jolly dies of dysentery and Holly, speeding out to nurse him, marries Val and stays in South Africa.

Back in England, young Jolyon marries Irene and there is news that they have a son, named Jon. Soames marries Annette, hiding from the family anything about that restaurant in Soho; in due time, she too is to have a child. But her travail comes prematurely. Soames, distraught in his house at Mapledurham, has to decide on the alternatives presented to him by the doctor—operate and lose the child, or refrain from an operation and save the child but risk losing the mother; if she lives, in either case there can be no more children. He decides not to operate, but make sure of the child. When it is born, the mother too survives but the child is a daughter (to be named Fleur). Soames has scarcely time to contemplate the bitterness of this—no son to carry on his name and no chance of another child from his wife—for his very old father, James, lies dying in his house in Park Lane and he must hurry to his deathbed. Before the old man dies, Soames comforts him by lying about the child—yes, a son. Then he sombrely returns to Mapledurham, gravely contemplates the new-born and suddenly feels deep love for this child flowing into him. The book ends with the sentence, "By God! this—this thing was his."

When the novel was published in October 1920, it was received with the respect which Galsworthy by then commanded, but no critic perceived the essential change that had taken place in the conception of the Forsytes and of the author's whole attitude to property, including even property of the person; for he recognizes with sympathy Soames's desire for a son and for the first time Irene's loathing of the man she had married assumes a little of the taint of unreasonableness. Because Irene was Ada, Galsworthy had from the start avoided any interpretation of her feelings. In *The Man of Property*, as he himself pointed out, she never takes the stage but is always seen by some other person; she is the disturbing essence of beauty, the catalyst that without any sort of change in itself (or indeed any explanation of itself), is added to the experiment entirely for the change it will produce in others. Had he developed the character of Irene as he developed that of his other principal figures, he would necessarily have had to explain why she loathed Soames (long before he committed the act of legal rape against her), instead of simply stating that she did. It may be that he avoided this, not wholly for artistic reasons—effective though the device is artistically— but because it would have implied an explanation of why Ada disliked Major Arthur. That explanation would have been, if truthfully faced by Galsworthy, much closer to the merely ordinary and sordid than he would dare to admit to himself.

Certainly Irene's lack of substance in the novels eased the task of forgiving and gradually coming to sympathize with Soames, which was essential if the *Saga* was to be continued by an author who had returned to the world of convention, power, respectability, and indeed property. In 1920, even that acute critic, C. E. Montague, writing in the *Manchester Guardian*, could not perceive the change that had occurred. He saw that the "abhorred Soames" was no longer treated with abhorrence but he felt that Galsworthy, "in all the quintessentially good breeding of his art and the delicate sincerity of his heart and mind", had simply returned to the manner of *The Country House*, with its "almost disconcerting equity in which even cruel and gross people are seen as they might be by one who had known them as children learning to walk".

This was not really what had happened at all. Even *The Country House*, for all its charm, had been written in a spirit of anger at society. But *In Chancery* was written with a touch of gentle anger—perhaps no more than a reproving glance—at that which would disrupt society. This was the new basic theme, to be developed ever more strongly as the *Chronicles* continued, which would allow Galsworthy to identify himself ever more securely with his central character, the once-abhorred Soames.

Before *In Chancery* was published, Galsworthy had already finished the short linking story and the third novel, which were to complete the *Saga*. He had begun them in Spain towards the end of 1919. In November he and Ada had gone to Oxford and ascended Boar's Hill on a foggy day to see the Masefields and the Gilbert Murrays. Much less than this, of course, sufficed to give Ada a cold and by the time they started their usual winter journey abroad she was in full distress. All December they had to stay in the Hotel Louvois in Paris, where she developed neuritis of the jaws and ears and for two days was unable even to put her head to a pillow but had to sit continuously upright. For a fortnight she went deaf. "Till the end of the month," he noted, "great pain for A., strenuous nursing for me." Just after Christmas, however, the pain was alleviated and a young English doctor gave an assurance that the deafness was caused merely by neuritis of the nerves and would shortly pass off. So they left for Biarritz and then Spain, where they feasted themselves on the Goyas in Madrid and the sunshine which at last they found in Seville, before moving on to Malaga and Algeciras. In spite of his sickroom duties, he had found time in Paris and Biarritz to write the short linking story, "Awakening", which, with a description of the nine-year-old childhood at Robin Hill of Jon (Irene's and young Jolyon's son), brings the family story forward to 1909. It is one of the worst examples of the sudden swamps of sentimentality into which Galsworthy was now occasionally to stagger. Because of these, the charge of general sentimentality has often been levelled at him, but unjustly. To the end of his writing career the basic ground upon which he strode was hard, realistic. The sentimentality was confined to a few grossly over-written passages, of which "Awakening" is a prime example, mostly related to childhood and as in this instance to his own. Jon's childhood at Robin Hill is unquestionably a sickly recollection of Galsworthy's at Coombe Warren. Jon's longing for closer love from and understanding by his mother can only be an echo of Galsworthy's own childhood desires; the difference being that Jon gets from Irene the love which his author never received from Blanche.

So far as the *Saga* is concerned, however, "Awakening" is of scant importance. The narrative is not significantly renewed until the third novel of the trilogy, which Galsworthy began writing under the original title *For Ever*, altered before publication to *To Let*. He worked steadily at it all that winter in Spain, although Ada again fell sick with "flue" and bronchitis at Granada. Galsworthy had, until then, been rather enjoying the Alhambra, gipsy dancing, the countryside. "It certainly is a most ravishing place," he noted. "It is a great shame that it should have been so spoiled for us both." By the end of March Ada was well enough to begin the homeward journey, though the train to Madrid nearly floored her again —there was a railway strike, so the train travelled by devious and long back ways, taking twenty-four hours to arrive. She gamely struggled to the Prado for another look at the Goyas, but by the time Galsworthy got her home to Grove Lodge in Hampstead she was ready to take to her bed for six weeks, during which Galsworthy worked hard at the rehearsals of *The Skin Game* at St Martin's Theatre. Ada was not well enough to attend the first night.

Towards the end of May they went to Wingstone and he resumed the full flow of writing *To Let*, breaking off only to attend the Eton and Harrow match, a sacred function for him. He finished the draft on September 5, 1920. Then he and Ada returned to Hampstead, where he revised it just in time to get it to the publisher before they set off once more to winter in America.

With *To Let*, Galsworthy jumped the Forsytes over the war into the year 1920—the year in which, in fact, he was writing it. Indeed, when he began the novel in Malaga it was only January of that year, but the book itself opens with Soames Forsyte emerging "from the Knightsbridge Hotel, where he was staying, in the afternoon of the 12th of May, 1920, with the intention of visiting a collection of pictures in a Gallery off Cork Street, and looking into the Future".

The future, for Soames, is his daughter Fleur; and he meets it at once in the picture gallery that June Forsyte is running on behalf of her lame-duck artists, where it happens that, as Soames brings his daughter, Irene brings her son Jon. These two, knowing nothing of the old animosities between her father and his mother, fall in love. Soames, though doubting, tries to smooth the path for them, since that is what Fleur wants. Young Jolyon wants to tell the boy, as soon as he knows of his love for Fleur, that her father once owned his mother like a slave, but Irene cannot bear to let him know. At last Jolyon must tell the boy; and, having told him, dies of a failing heart. Despite all Fleur's scheming—in part, because of Fleur's scheming—Jon tells her that they can never come together now. Soames's act of property, performed so many years ago, has exacted its retribution. The boy takes his mother away to Canada. Fleur, no longer caring what she does, marries Michael Mont, a baronet's son who is in love with her but for whom she feels nothing but thin affection. In the background, the Victorian Forsyte era is coming to an end; Timothy, the last of the old generation, now a hundred years old, dies in his house in the Bayswater Road. Only Soames, Gradman, the old clerk to the firm of solicitors, and the domestic servants appear at his funeral in the family grave at Highgate. It is at Highgate that the book and the *Saga* splendidly end, with Soames in the cemetery, paying a solitary visit to the family vault, musing on the end of the old Forsytes and his own life, and knowing that "he might wish and wish and never get it—the beauty and the loving in the world". The retribution through the suffering of his daughter, the only person whom he now loves, is no longer that of satire but of tragedy. At that moment Soames is purged of the last vestige of "abhorrence" and becomes the completely sympathetic tragic hero punished, in spite of his good intentions, by fate.

It was then that Galsworthy could write to Harley Granville-Barker that the *Saga*, when published in one volume, would be "my passport, however difficult it may be to get it viséd, for the shores of permanence". But in the same year he could write to Chevrillon that "though the *Saga* is finished—the old Forsytes all gone—and the long duel over, I feel that I haven't done with Fleur; and am trying to gather force to pursue her in the world of today and tomorrow".

He himself had not quite understood, at that time, that it

was not Fleur who would persuade him to continue, but Soames; that Soames, purged now by suffering, stood ready to step completely into his author's shoes and to represent his attitudes to the world that he saw around him and no longer—save in that which was new and brash—actively disliked.

But that was still for the future. The present was vivid enough. Even before the publication of *The Forsyte Saga* in a single volume, Galsworthy was accepted as among the leading men of letters of his country, in a period that embraced Shaw, Wells, Conrad, Bennett, Hardy, Masefield, James. When the P.E.N. Club was founded, he was chosen as its President—a post which he, at any rate, took with immense seriousness and for which he worked with selfless assiduity for the rest of his life. As his works were collected into a limited edition for publication in Britain and America, a cycle of his plays was put on in London. To chime with this importance and dignity, Ada had for some years been carefully dissuading even his oldest friends from addressing him any longer as "Jack"; they now wrote their letters to a friendly, but formal, "J.G." (It was not, however, until after his death that she engaged the College of Heralds to make him a coat of arms.)

His importance as a man of letters was now accepted throughout the world. When he travelled abroad, he received the sort of public acclaim that it is difficult to imagine any writer now receiving. When, for instance he and Ada went to Scandinavia in the spring of 1922 for Galsworthy to deliver a lecture on Dickens, Turgeniev and Maupassant, they were received by the British Ambassador in Copenhagen, taken to supper by the Crown Prince in Stockholm and next day given a formal luncheon by him at the Palace, attended by the diplomatic corps and the most eminent men of Sweden. For his lecture, Nansen took the chair.

To some extent, this was still the acclaim of the world of

letters and of the universities. But when *The Forsyte Saga* was published as a single volume on May 25, 1922, Galsworthy became also a public figure. In both Britain and America the single volume ran at once into best-selling figures. The writer who had never betrayed his literary integrity as he saw it—though, certainly, with the comfortable backing of a substantial private income—suddenly found himself also a popular author. The austerity with which he had encompassed himself did not in the least diminish; indeed, it still further served to advance the very reason of his popularity, his Englishness. For his new-found readers it was obviously preferable that he should be and should remain a figure of aloofness: the English gentleman, in terms nevertheless that everybody could understand and, what is more, enjoy.

The contemporary judgment on the *Saga* has not been reversed and will not be. In spite of the sudden change of outlook, of character, of purpose, between *The Man of Property* and all that follows, the *Saga* taken as a whole stands among the dozen or so important works of English fiction of this century. Siegfried Sassoon wrote, when he finished reading it, "I take off my hat to him and all his Forsytes; that that family is becoming a part of the national consciousness, I am surer than ever." It is indeed this, of all Galsworthy's voluminous works, that can stake his claim for permanence. In its Englishness, its breadth of humanity and the fine simplicity of its language, it ranks among the great national novels— with *Vanity Fair*, say, or *Oliver Twist*, or *Tom Jones*. Conrad's exclamation at it was just, *"Oeuvre de poète!"*

XXII

After his father's death, John Galsworthy regarded himself as patriarch of his family, scrupulously honouring the duties of that position. To his brother Hubert, who was not blessed with much worldly success, he always held out whatever help was needed. His sister Mabel (she of the June Forsyte qualities of impetuousness and the nurturing of lame ducks) was closely in his affection throughout his life and to his nephews and nieces he was invariably warm and generous. He set up Hubert's son, young Hubert, on a poultry farm near Winchester. In his will he created a trust of his possessions and copyrights, leaving the income to Ada in her lifetime and afterwards in five equal shares to the five children of his brother and sisters. It was a considerable trust, for his estate was proved at £95,283 12s. 11d. gross; nearly as great a fortune as his father's in actual figures though not, of course, in purchasing power.

Of all his family, those to whom he was specially devoted were his sister Lilian Sauter, her son Rudolf and Viola Brookman, the girl who had lived with and sustained Lilian when Rudo was interned in the closing months of the war, and whom he later married. Lilian, with her deep seriousness about art and her steel determination in so fragile a body, had been the most respected companion of Galsworthy's childhood; her marriage to the Bavarian painter had strongly influenced him as a young man to make something more of his life than mere affluent idleness; and the disastrous break-up of that marriage by Sauter's internment, followed by the internment of Rudo, aroused in Galsworthy a feeling of special devotion to those particular members of his family. When Rudo was at last freed in August 1919, he was sent at once to Wingstone with his mother and Vi, so that he might recover his balance and, indeed, his health. His release from internment by no means ended his difficulties, for his mother's property had been seized because of her marriage to an enemy national and was not easily freed. Galsworthy at once came to the Sauters' aid. He bought them a house for £2,000 in the north London suburb of Hendon and spent a further £1,000 on renovating it and fitting it up with a studio; Rudo intended to devote his life, as his father had done, to painting. When Rudo protested at his uncle's generosity, he wrote to him, "Dear old man, the one thing fatal in the adjustment of all our lives to the new circumstances of the times before us will be that unnecessary and dangerous creature, the high horse. And there's one thing specially that you and your mother should remember. Your Grandfather intended his children and their offspring to share his money *equally*. If the Government is so un-English as to deprive or sequestrate the English property of an English-blooded person, to pay the claims of another English-blooded person, it behoves me, who am blessed by Providence, to see that my Father's sacred wishes, for which he laboured all his life, are not upset to any material extent. Your Mother is not fit to rough it, and it will only handicap you all to try the experiment. . . . Having no children, you see, we are bound to look on you with a special eye; and it would be in the nature of the ridiculous for you to stand on ceremony with us in material matters. . . . Hang it all, I am your wicked Uncle. . . . When I was your age I didn't spurn my Father. I took all I could get from him, and look where I am now, paying goodness knows what in super-tax. Towards you I am my Father personified—don't spurn us."

Accepting this situation, the Sauters settled into the Hendon house, Rudo and Vi getting married. In 1923 he painted a portrait of Galsworthy as he sat in an armchair at Grove

Lodge correcting the proofs of the limited edition of his works, the portrait of a successful and assured man. As a companion to it, Rudo then made a portrait of his mother at Freeland, as they had called the Hendon house. It is unmistakably a portrait of suffering. Lilian is no longer the ethereal almost translucent figure whom Georg Sauter had painted so delicately in those long-past prewar days, after a visit to the high mountains, to the spiritual atmosphere of which she always responded. Her son's is the portrait of an unhappy, frail, heart-broken woman; and indeed she never recovered from the severing of her marriage. This was reflected in an increasing bodily fragility. In the late summer of 1924 she contracted pleurisy but seemed to have recovered from it. Her brother arranged for her to be taken by ambulance and then in the Blue Train for convalescence in Austria. Suddenly she had a heart attack and died. In spite of the depth of his own grief—it was a year, too, which had been saddened by the death of Conrad—Galsworthy's chief thought was for Rudo and Vi, especially as Rudo had scarcely himself recovered from a recent operation. He could not offer them the sanctuary of Wingstone, since he had now given up his tenancy of that farmhouse—or, rather, of the half of it which had been for so long his country home. He had relinquished it without much regret because the dampness of the house and its situation, he had decided, were not doing Ada's rheumatism any good. In fact, she did not like the place. She did not really like living in the country at all and suffered it only because Galsworthy could not properly imagine *anybody* wanting to live permanently in a town; though, in truth, Ada did—shops, theatres, concert halls were her idea of things, not fields and trees. Because, therefore, Galsworthy could not at that time provide his nephew with a refuge in the country, he at once invited him and Vi to accompany Ada and himself on their customary winter journey abroad, upon which they were just about to start. The previous winter they had spent in Madeira and Biarritz. This one they were proposing to devote to Italy, then North Africa. The Galsworthys went ahead to Merano, where the Sauters joined them, to find Ada already in bed with a severe cold. Rudo at once started painting and held long discussions with his uncle on the theory of that art. By December, when Ada had sufficiently recovered, they travelled south through Rome, and thence to Syracuse, where the weather was unaccountably wet and cold and Ada's bronchial state therefore the worse. She confessed to self-annoyance at taking up so much of Galsworthy's time but added, "Of course there is no choice about it, and the tiny consolation is that he has a genius for nursing and does really enjoy coffee-making, milk-boiling and all such games."

In spite of all such difficulties, he was already nearly half-way through the second Forsyte trilogy which, when finally published in a single volume with the title *A Modern Comedy*, would complete *The Forsyte Chronicles*. He had already completed and published the first novel of the new trilogy, *The White Monkey*, having begun it in Hampstead in November 1922, continued it in the Italian Tyrol during the summer of 1923 and finished it while he and Ada were staying in Madeira and then in Portugal during the following winter. By the spring of 1924 it was being serialized in magazines in both Britain and the United States, and Galsworthy was begging his friends not to read it in that form but to wait the publication of the volume in the autumn of that year.

The White Monkey was the beginning of that pursuit of Fleur Forsyte "into the world of today and tomorrow" about which he had earlier written to Chevrillon. The opening scenes of the book, indeed, are those of Fleur creating a smart *salon* in her house in Westminster, taking part in all the brittle life of the youth of the early 'twenties, and regarded with a satiric, slightly disapproving eye by her husband, Michael

Mont, now a publisher, as well as by Galsworthy himself. He had by then reversed his attitude towards marriage and sex. He depicts Fleur Mont as, having married without love, being attracted by a young wartime poet, Wilfred Desert, who is passionately devoted to her. This is very nearly Ada's situation in the 1890s. But in 1922 Galsworthy has little sympathy for the lover. There is no more flouting the world and going where the heart calls. All his sympathy is with Michael, the husband, who is goodness and kindness itself, and with the conventions of society; Fleur emerges as a somewhat despicable, slightly sordid young woman.

When *The White Monkey* was published, the surprising discovery that the ageing Galsworthy (by then fifty-seven) could understand the wildness and intellectual freedom of the generation of young people liberated from war caused most comment. But at this distance of time these opening chapters fade into comparative dullness and the novel does not come to life until Chapter Six, in which Soames Forsyte reappears. At once it is evident that the novel and indeed probably the whole trilogy is to be about him, not Fleur. It would have been an inconsiderable novel had it concerned itself only with Fleur's hesitant rejection of the poet, Desert, and her return to Michael to bear his child; or with Michael Mont's humane attempts to smooth over the troubles of a young fellow dismissed for a trifling theft into a London of misery and unemployment and to reconcile him to his wife who has secretly become an artists' model to earn enough to get them both away to the sunshine and the hopefulness of Australia. What makes the book is Soames, mousing forward into the modern world with his Victorian standards, now thoroughly approved by his creator. It is he who, visiting the deathbed of his cousin George, the only other surviving Forsyte of his generation, sees on the wall the Chinese painting of a white monkey and buys it at the sale to present to his daughter for her Chinese room—the symbol of erring humanity in any age, this white monkey with strangely human eyes, which is "eating the fruit, scattering the rind, and being copped at it". It is Soames Forsyte who now speaks for Galsworthy's own sense of values, contrasted with the cynicism of Michael's father, Sir Lawrence Mont. The chief narrative interest of the novel is Soames's venture on to the board of a City insurance company, threatened by the sudden collapse of the German mark. At this sort of story Galsworthy was compulsive. By far the finest thing in the book is the scene in which the board confront the shareholders and Soames, whose honesty of principle has compelled the scandal to be dragged out into the open, challenges with contempt the accusations that they level at him and dismisses from his life the whole of dubious modern business morality. Henceforth he will merely defend his own for the sake of his daughter and his new grandson and, for interest, will become a notable collector of pictures.

With *The White Monkey* published and respectfully acclaimed before he set off for the winter journey with Ada and the Sauters, Galsworthy was already embarked on the writing of the second volume of the trilogy, to be called *The Silver Spoon*; and was finding the work difficult. Ada's illness was not the only distraction. While they were in Sicily, Georg Sauter came across from Venice to meet his son and daughter-in-law for the first time since the war. By January, however, he was concentrating on the novel, which he read out loud of an evening to his companions when new chapters were ready; on other evenings they got *The Pickwick Papers*. Towards the end of the month they crossed the Mediterranean into Tunisia and Algeria, then travelled to Fez and Marrakech, *The Silver Spoon* and *Pickwick* sharing the desert evenings. Skirting the zone of battle between the Spaniards and the Riffs, they returned to Spain via Tangier. The end of the journey was marred by Vi's going down with an attack of paratyphoid.

Shortly after they returned to England Galsworthy was also attacked. They concluded that he and Vi had contracted the disease from a plate of radishes in Marrakech which the two others had not eaten.

All four of them spent the summer of 1925 in London at Grove Lodge and Freeland. Galsworthy was still hard at work on *The Silver Spoon*, a novel that seems to have slowed him down more than usual. He had finished it, however, by November when it was time for the winter journey abroad. This year it was to be America again and they took Rudo and Vi, who were to be their companions on the annual trek for the rest of Galsworthy's life. By now it was accepted that they had taken the place in his affections of the children he had never had. He had particular affection and esteem for Rudo. In his will he appointed him an executor, and also successor to Ada as his literary representative, entrusted with the care of his writings.

They spent most of that winter in Arizona and California, with Galsworthy reading aloud in the evenings, as had now become routine, but from a more widely varied repertory— *Treasure Island*, *Catriona*, *Ballantrae* and Shakespeare's sonnets. Rudo painted a portrait of Ada, now a middle-aged woman with very much the appearance of an American matron, seated in a fantail-backed high chair in an hotel lounge. Galsworthy wrote a play, *Escape*. He declared it was the last he intended to write, though in fact he wrote two more and had begun a third at the time of his death. *Escape*, however, was his last great theatrical success (neither of the two following plays amounts to anything much by any standards). It illumined for him the summer of 1926 and ran for a year. Only a few days after it opened *The Silver Spoon* was published. There had been a lapse of time when nothing much except a collected volume of short stories and an indifferent play had appeared from Galsworthy's pen. But this sudden re-emergence with play and novel in August and September of 1926 brought him firmly back into public attention, though *The Silver Spoon* was not only received rather more tepidly than the earlier Forsyte novels but sold rather more slowly, as though there was stealing in a slight public weariness of the family chronicle.

Yet *The Silver Spoon* is a stronger, better contrived novel than its predecessor. In all these later novels, in which technical skill was more evident than deep personal emotion, Galsworthy established as the centre of his narrative a conflict of a kind more likely to furnish a drama than a novel, but so adroitly handled as to compel the reader to follow it through to the end. In *The Silver Spoon*, the central conflict is a libel action brought against Fleur by Marjorie Ferrar, the dissolute young granddaughter of an earl. The action arises from a sneer, overheard by Soames, that Fleur is a lion-hunter and a snob. Much of the rest of the book is a somewhat tedious exposition of Galsworthy's pet and personal remedies for the economic and social ills of England in the 'twenties, about which he was continually worrying; briefly, he wanted a revival of the country's agriculture, and the planned emigration of surplus children to the colonies. In order to expound these unrealistic ideas, he retired Michael Mont from his publishing house and sent him into Parliament. But the central conflict of the libel action, with the defence cunningly turned at Soames's instigation into an attack upon the dissolute morals of the contemporary young men and women of intellect and wealth, is story-telling at Galsworthy's finest. At the end, when Marjorie Ferrar has lost her action and been exposed as a loose woman before the world of London, it is not she who is cold-shouldered, but Fleur; as Michael has foreseen, the very defence that saved the action was bound to identify her with the prim and the smug. Because it is basically Soames who has done this to his daughter, out of sheer love for her, it is he who offers to take her off on a voyage round the world, leaving Michael to complete, meanwhile, the political tasks to which he has set himself. The marriage, clearly, is near to breaking-point.

Since *The Man of Property*, and *The Country House*, Galsworthy had not written a more skilful novel than this, in spite of its somewhat tiresome political background. He must have felt the inadequacy of its reception, which was little more than respectful, although he showed no sign in the letters he wrote at that time of being aware of any lack of warmth for his book. Perhaps it was more than compensated for by the success of *Escape*. Or perhaps Galsworthy had by then settled so completely into the role of a public figure, an eminent man of letters, that he took even faint praise as homage due.

XXIII

In the latter half of 1926, Galsworthy established the final pattern of his life. He had earlier suggested to Rudo and Vi Sauter that they should sell Freeland, the house at Hendon which was now being engulfed in waves of suburbia, and he would buy them a house in the country, where they could live permanently and where Galsworthy and Ada could keep a suite of rooms for themselves, just as they had at Wingstone. The Sauters therefore set off to search for a suitable house, to a price limit which their uncle had imposed of £3,000. They started at Rye and worked eastwards to Arundel, marking down houses that might suit. Then all four drove again over the route to look at these houses but Ada disliked something or other about each of them. After two rather despairing days they were lunching at Pulborough when Vi said she would just try the local house agent to see if anything else were on offer. All he could suggest was Bury House, about halfway between Pulborough and Arundel, which had been built in Tudor style on the site of an earlier house that had burned down. It contained twenty-two rooms, and most of the fifteen bedrooms had separate little triangular baths in cupboard-like compartments. The asking price was £9,000. Since they had nothing else to do with the afternoon, they drove along to see it. It was a modern manor, faced with grey stone, with mullioned windows and a slab roof. But when Galsworthy walked round it and came upon the view of Bury Hill to one side and Amberley downs to the other, he said, "This is the place. I like this."

Rudo, horrified at the thought of trying to run such an immense house, tried to dissuade him. But he would not be moved. He would not, of course, expect Rudo and Vi to take on such a responsibility; they would simply reverse the original idea and Galsworthy himself would buy and live in the house with Ada. Rudo and Vi would come to live there with them. He returned to Pulborough and told the astonished house agent that he would pay the asking price (he disliked haggling, says Rudo). Within less than two months they had furnished the place and moved in. On the very day of the move, a lorry driver who lived in a cottage over the road was killed in an accident. Galsworthy at once bought his cottage and sent Vi over to tell the widow she could live there rent free for as long as she liked and draw all her vegetables from the garden at Bury House. Before long, he bought all the cottages he could get hold of in the village—nine in all—and put in bathrooms and other amenities they lacked. He could not understand the air of suspicion and antipathy he met in the village, until it was explained to him that the tenants all thought their rents were going up. Horrified, he sent Vi along to assure them all that the rents would be reduced. Money, he once told Vi, he regarded simply as a means of doing things without having to worry about financing them. Rudo sometimes thought that this particular act was, perhaps subconsciously, a gesture of contrition for some of the house property from which part of the fortune he inherited from his father had in the first place been drawn.

Thus in the opening months of his sixtieth year, having toiled unremittingly at the art and craft of writing for slightly more than half that period of time, Galsworthy set himself up, with his house in London and his mansion in Sussex, in a style suited to the eminence he had reached. Not that the toil was in the least remitted. He had still to complete the huge task of *The Forsyte Chronicles*. That done, there was to be yet another family chronicle, in yet another trilogy. Throughout the winter journey, which all four of them took in 1926-27 in South

Africa, without much of any event happening, he was writing laboriously the third volume of A *Modern Comedy*, to be the end of the Forsytes and to be entitled *Swan Song*. The only alterations in the usual run of their lives which Rudo noted in South Africa were that, for once, Ada was completely well and that Galsworthy himself was more reserved than ever, seeming to draw farther into himself. In the evenings he read, but no longer out loud. Rudo, puzzled, noted in his diary, "I am afraid either he is getting more and more apathetic and uninterested in both people and things, or he is disgruntled with us. Certainly, I've been as grumpy as a bear, but it's mostly the work [his painting], and anyway I don't mean it."

Perhaps, after all, Galsworthy's mood rose simply from the atmosphere of South Africa itself, which he did not find congenial. For when they returned to England in the spring, all four settled at once into Bury House and Galsworthy resumed in full the pleasant and dignified life for which he had now established the setting.

The days at Bury ran to a pattern. Before breakfast, Galsworthy and Rudo rode together on the downs. Galsworthy remained a fearless horseman, although galloping across the downs carried hazards which could at his age have been serious. Every morning, however, there came a moment when he touched at the reins and his companion knew that he was wildly away.

Breakfast was formal and lengthy, as were all the meals at Bury House. It lasted for at least one hour, during which Galsworthy opened his mail and discussed it. At half past ten he and Ada took the correspondence to the billiards room and spread it on the billiards table. Then he paced the room, dictating, and she took down his replies in longhand; he would never have a personal letter typed. She was very deft at all this and very swift: she had an envelope addressed while he was thinking of the next phrase, and so on. When all the personal letters were finished, Ada took the rest upstairs, and there proceeded to type his current manuscript. She herself typed the first three drafts of all his work and only the fourth, which was to go to the printer, was sent to a professional typing agency.

When she had gone, Galsworthy settled to his morning's composition, either in the billiards room, on the terrace outside or occasionally in his study at the top of the house. He wrote, as always, on a block of paper balanced on his knee, using a J nib and a bottle of ink, and always with a dog lying at his feet. He continued to write throughout the morning, long after Ada had finished her typing and set out with Vi to take the other dogs for a walk across the fields. He rarely laid down his pen until it was time for lunch—once again a formal meal, though of a simple kind if there were no guests in the house.

Galsworthy devoted the afternoons to Ada. They usually spent it playing croquet, in a long series of games which, of course, he contrived that she usually won. Sometimes he and Rudo would have a singles at tennis. Galsworthy had taken up tennis in his fifties, during one of his winter sojourns abroad and, for a man of his age, had come to play with considerable skill. He was unconventional but cunning; difficult to beat even though he had not much in the way of strokes or pace. He and Ada were then ready for tea, after which he settled to revision of the manuscript upon which he was then working or correction of the proofs of the book preceding or writing an article for a newspaper or magazine. Dinner, for which everybody dressed whether there were guests or not, was at eight o'clock and was an elaborate meal, lasting usually for an hour and a half. Before dinner he offered everybody a glass of sherry; he would never allow cocktails. The meal itself was, of course, accompanied by wine and followed by brandy. Then there was the evening to pass. Sometimes they played billiards.

Sometimes Galsworthy sat desultorily reading while, in the same room, Ada and Rudo played duets, she on the piano, he on the flute. Often Galsworthy nodded off drowsily over his book and sometimes roused himself again to ask for the piece of music that had just been played. When the evening was at last, happily, coming to an end, he settled down on a sofa with all the dogs around him and the maids brought in a pot of tea, or whisky if anybody wanted it. Every evening he stood up at about eleven o'clock and went outside to stare for several minutes at the sky. This contemplation of nature by night, before going to his bed, had become a ritual, perhaps of an almost religious kind, which he never omitted when he was in the country.

Life at Bury House was somewhat formal, gracious, unimaginative and somewhat costly (though Galsworthy never spent in any year even what was left of his income after deducting his charitable gifts). But it was not run on a large household staff. He would never have manservants about the house but insisted on pretty, fresh-looking maids; there were only parlourmaid and housemaid, always recruited from the same family, living in a nearby village on the Arundel estate. The cook was slow and backward (and not, it seems, a very good cook), but he insisted on keeping her because of her devotion to Vi. He could not, in any case, bear to dismiss an employee. Although two of the five gardeners were felt by Vi and Ada to be so incompetent that they ought to be sacked, he refused. There were two million unemployed in the country, he pointed out, and where could the men hope to get another job? He was always trying to arrange his life to be of help to other people—quite genuinely and without any thought of its being known. When he first arrived at Bury House he doubled the wages of all the gardeners. That did become known and aroused a lot of protest from the county. It was not only towards his underlings, however, that he was so considerate and thoughtful: he was not acting from any motives of inverted snobbery. He was equally anxious to study the wants of the guests, mostly from the worlds of literature or the stage, who filled Bury House each weekend. When, for example, Barrie came to stay, he always kept his bedroom light burning all night. This was unfortunate, since the house made its own electricity, a single lamp kept the engine running and by morning it was always overheated. Galsworthy would not embarrass Barrie by mentioning this to him or providing him with an oil lamp or anything of that kind; he simply had a second engine installed, to take over on the nights when Barrie was staying at the house.

Life at Grove Lodge in Hampstead was of much the same pattern as at Bury House, except that in London Galsworthy had committees, rehearsals and theatres to attend, leaving him less time for drowsing over books to the accompaniment of piano and flute duets. In Hampstead there were two domestics who, for years before the war, had been Lilian Sauter's servants. Galsworthy took them on and they worked for him for the remainder of his life and for Ada after his death; when, after the war, one of them married an ex-soldier, Galsworthy had him taught to drive a car and took him on too as chauffeur.

But whether sleepily at Bury House, or busily in London, life always contained his morning's writing. In 1927 he had published two short *Forsyte Interludes* to form links between the three novels of his trilogy. He had already finished the writing of the third novel, *Swan Song*, which was published in July 1928, some months after the Galsworthys and the Sauters had returned from a less ambitious winter journey to the south of France. Although the trilogy, thus completed, was not to be published in a single volume as A *Modern Comedy* for another year, *Swan Song* alone completely repaired whatever failing of public interest in the Forsytes there may have been. The central theme is the return to England, at the time of the General Strike in 1926, of Jon Forsyte, now married to his American, and Fleur's realization that she still hungers for him. She plans and carries out his seduction in the coppice at Robin Hill where so much of the old story was worked out. The corollary to having possessed him is then, of course, that she must at once lose him. When Soames sees her distraught at the realization, he carries her off to his house at Mapledurham, unfailing in his love, but helpless. That night, without knowing what she is doing, Fleur accidentally sets fire with a cigarette to the picture gallery of the house. It is during his fevered efforts to save his pictures that Soames thrusts her from the death he sees she is deliberately courting from a heavy falling frame, takes the blow himself and, in a few days, dies.

Galsworthy had not at first intended to kill him off. "He will survive this book," he wrote to Granville-Barker in April 1927. "I purport killing him in a final outburst, but I expect he will outlive me yet. At present he's so young, you know —a mere seventy-two." But as he came to the end of the narrative, he understood that nothing but Soames's death could round off the *Chronicles*, and he wrote once again to Granville-Barker, telling him for his private ear—"*Le Roi est mort.*" Galsworthy, for whom Soames had become the fictional representative, had no more to say about the society in which he had been brought up and in which he still dwelt. The bitterness had long since evaporated. The whole concept of middle-class standards had become, he felt, irrelevant to an England he scarcely any longer understood. So Soames died, and with him ended the career of John Galsworthy as a writer of importance; there would be more to come, much more, but none of it would say any more than he had already said and would not say it so well.

At that point, however, he had written, starting with the

first impulse of his own love for Ada, a continuous family chronicle of some three-quarters of a million words—something not to be found anywhere else in English literature. It is easy to fault it. The original theme was reversed. It is uneven in quality. There are patches of gross sentimentality, though they are less frequent than some critics have declared. It is marred by snobbism, by cranky political preachings, by an irritating air of condescension towards the lower classes. It is easy to cast doubts on the picture of England that is drawn in the Chronicles from the 1880s to the 1920s, or even to question the veracity of the chief characters (Gilbert Murray had the perceptiveness to remark, at the end of the Saga, "the rum thing to me is that, after reading it all and admiring and loving it, I don't feel that I know in the least what a Forsyte is like, and I am not conscious of having seen one").

But when all the faults have been noted, all the doubts mooted, The Forsyte Chronicles remain an outstanding—perhaps the outstanding—work of English fiction of the twentieth century, and, certainly, the most English novel of our days. The work of a giant.

XXIV

The completion of *The Forsyte Chronicles* was the signal for honours to be pressed upon their author. Already possessed of a doctorate from Manchester and an honorary degree from Princeton—accepted on his behalf by Charles Scribner—he was soon also to get doctorates from Dublin, Cambridge, Sheffield and his own university of Oxford. To this academic honouring of a now international figure the nation itself added its highest recognition. In the Birthday Honours of June 1929, he was entered into the Order of Merit. It was some reciprocation, Herbert Samuel wrote to him, of the dignity which he had conferred upon contemporary English literature. With a judicious sense of timing, he had just offered the complete manuscript of the *Chronicles* (except for that of *The Man of Property*, which he had long ago destroyed) to the British Museum. The manuscript of *Strife* was already safely lodged in the Bodleian; that of *Loyalties* had fetched £3,300 at auction for the Royal Literary Fund; and Galsworthy was in consultation with Gabriel Wells, its purchaser, to see if it could not be arranged for *Justice*, say, to find a lasting home in the Morgan Library in America.

The steady course of his life continued between Bury House in the summer, Grove Lodge, and the interminable winter travelling abroad, always now accompanied by the Sauters. They made one disastrous journey to Brazil; the climate was insufferable and they returned as speedily as they decently could to Biarritz. The next winter they tried a couple of months in Majorca, which suited Ada's chest better but was dull, so they were not sorry to come back faithfully to Biarritz once more. The winter journeys were interspersed with short trips in summer to various parts of Europe; but these were now usually on P.E.N. business which Galsworthy still indefatigably pursued. In the winter of 1930-31 they made the last of their many journeys to America, a happy and successful one, during which Galsworthy delivered some lectures, Rudo exhibited some paintings, they visited many old friends, Ada remained in good health, they throve in the sunshine of Arizona and Galsworthy and Ada amused themselves by attempting a joint translation of *Carmen*. They came back from America much restored.

Just as Galsworthy's life ran throughout these years to the steady pattern he had set for it, so did the course of his writing. He was by then so confirmed in the habit of the morning stint that nothing short of incapacity could have prevented a large output, month by month, year by year. He was writing and publishing at a rate and volume that most novelists in their prime would find formidable. What is astonishing is the consistent standard of the work. He was not again, except in a few occasional, happy moments, to gain the heights he had reached in the best passages of the *Chronicles*, but never (except in his last, somewhat faltering work for the theatre) did he drop below a level that would have made a new reputation for another man.

Most of the occasional felicities came in a last backward look at the earlier Forsytes, a glance over the shoulder before moving away, in a volume of short stories, *On Forsyte Change*. The stories were all written after Galsworthy had finished *Swan Song* but they fill in little gaps in the much earlier history of the various members of the Forsyte family, ranging from Aunt Hester's one abortive love affair with a German officer when making a tour of the Rhine as a young woman in 1845, to the last story in the volume, "Soames and the Flag", an account of Soames's reaction to the Great War (in effect, Galsworthy's reaction to it), which is the last he was ever to write about the central character of his fiction. In some ways, this story is a more fitting end to the intimate relationship between Soames and his author than the death scene at the end of *Swan Song*. In this retrospective sketch, Galsworthy identifies Soames almost completely with himself, even to his inability to talk to anybody outside his close family circle on any but the most ordinary of topics. In this final glimpse of Soames there is no rancour left at all, not a jot of memory of the torture of Ada's first marriage, not a hint of rebellion; merely a warm portrait of his author, with all his liberal nature and love of his fellow beings shuddering at the brutal impact of the slaughter in France but maintaining at home the essential Englishness of character that does not permit the nation to lose final battles.

The volume of Forsyte stories, however, was only to fill the brief pause while Galsworthy gathered his strength to turn to his third and last trilogy of novels—*Maid in Waiting, Flowering Wilderness* and *Over the River*—the first two of which were separately published during his lifetime. The third, and all three gathered by Ada into a single volume with the title *End of the Chapter*, appeared only after his death.

These last three novels also make up a family chronicle, that of the family of Michael Mont's mother, the Charwells, or Cherrells as they are pronounced (and often, in the narrative, written). They are linked, therefore, quite considerably to *The Forsyte Chronicles*. Sir Lawrence Mont and Aunt Em, his wife, figure largely in the new novels; Hilary Charwell, the slum parson—Galsworthy's only sympathetic portrait of a clergyman—comes out more strongly in the new trilogy than in its predecessors; Wilfred Desert, the poet who fled to the East after Fleur had rejected his love, plays now a major part; and Michael and Fleur make perfunctory appearances.

But these links are irrelevant to Galsworthy's main purpose in *End of the Chapter*. Although the general strike had passed, the world was plunging into the great depression. He was deeply worried by the repercussions on England (he cared truly only for England), by the unemployment, the ruin of the countryside which he saw all round him and by the looming threat of a second world-wide war, fought disastrously from the skies, which he presciently felt already though there were as yet few hints of it nearer than China. From his seat at the head of the literary high table he felt it his duty to stress the value of service as a particularly English virtue which was in modern times being neglected. He chose as his subject, therefore, as in November 1930 he wrote to Chevrillon, "the older type of family with more tradition and sense of service than the Forsytes. I've finished one novel, and hope, if I have the luck, to write a trilogy on them. It's a stratum (the Service-manning stratum) that has been much neglected, and still exists in English life". Towards the end of the whole trilogy, he restated his theme thus, "So far the sense of social service was almost the perquisite of the older families who had somehow got hold of the notion that they must do something useful to pay for their position. Now that they were dying out, would a sense of service persist? How were the 'people' to take it up?"

The people most fit for the directive jobs, he earlier affirms, are those who have been born to the work, that is (to borrow a later phrase) the Establishment. It is a curious reversal of all he wrote in his youth in *The Island Pharisees*, the whole inspiration of which was a protest against that very conception of importance in the State. So far had a young man grown old, and success and recognition dulled and corrupted. Moreover, he made no attempt to depict the Cherrells as paragons. It is simply their service to the State that justifies favoured treatment for them, no matter what they have done; however sentimental Galsworthy may occasionally have been in the past, there is no sentimentality, but cynicism here. In *Maid in Waiting* a young officer, Hubert Cherrell, is threatened with punishment—perhaps even with deportation—on a charge of murder, for having shot in self-defence a mutinous Indian muledriver on an expedition of exploration in Bolivia. It seems quite proper to Galsworthy that high functionaries of State should most flagrantly pull strings to save the young man from any such retribution, for he is of a family that has served his country well for centuries and nobody must let that particular side down. *Flowering Wilderness*, the second novel, concerns the ill-starred love between Hubert's sister, Dinny, and Wilfred Desert, the poet; ill-starred because it becomes known that an Arab fanatic has forced Desert, at pistol point, to renounce Christianity and declare himself a Moslem. Although none of the Cherrells, not even the parson, is particularly religious, this act is condemned as cowardice and as a betrayal of the reputation of honour which enabled a few scattered Englishmen to hold in being an Empire of millions of lesser souls. When the old General, Dinny's father, hears of it, he bursts out with, "He'll be a pariah." The weight of opinion of men of his own kind—of the Services and of the clubs—forces Desert to flee from Dinny, flee from the country and seek oblivion and eventually death in distant jungles.

The last novel, *Over the River*, which falls well below the standard of the others, concerns the shuddering impact on the family of the divorce of Dinny's sister, Clare, by her sadist husband, a careerist in the Colonial Service. The Cherrell chronicle would have been better without this third book, for even Dinny herself, the last delightful character whom Galsworthy created—a young woman of integrity, charm and invincible honesty—is married off at the end of it, perfunctorily and quite unconvincingly, to a barrister so clumsily and unbelievably drawn that it is difficult to credit that the man who wrote him had lived for so long in the company of Soames and all the other Forsytes. But when Galsworthy was writing this book, he was already labouring under the weight of what seemed to be a growing weariness, lethargy, fatigue; afterwards it was to become apparent that he had written much of it while in the early stages of a mortal illness. He was by then seeing almost nobody, living like a recluse. Sometimes, when he laid down his pen after a morning's effort, he would say dispiritedly to Rudo, "Only one page this morning—I feel like a boy out of school"—that is, at the release that came from the hour for lunch. The last trilogy, which he had begun at Bury House in March 1928, and written there, in London, in America and in various hotels in Europe until he finished it at Bury House again on August 13, 1932—the day before his sixty-fifth birthday—seemed to his intimates to have exhausted him unduly. He, who had always felt a joy in writing, found it now a heavy task. Even in the publication of the only two novels of this last trilogy that appeared in his lifetime— *Maid in Waiting* in 1931 and *Flowering Wilderness* in November 1932—he took scant interest. The latter publication was, in any event, completely overshadowed by the last and greatest honour to be paid to him. On November 10 it was announced that he had been awarded the Nobel Prize for Literature. When a friend telephoned the news to Bury, it was brought to him in the garden, where he and Ada were having a game of croquet. "His brothers and sisters of the craft are not merely proud of him as winner of the Nobel prize," wrote Barrie, "but he makes us thereby a little prouder of ourselves, a privilege which many other bodies share with us, for he is ever doing service to humanity in general as well as to literature in particular."

"It is splendid that Sweden should have chosen an Englishman," Masefield wrote to him, "and glorious that she should have chosen you."

Granville-Barker wrote, "I like to think of you representing English letters to the world. For your England is my England, more or less; an England that I can explain and be proud of and (humanly) justify. . . . Like all true romancers, you've made a world of your own, which is the world of your idea. A complete world now, pretty well. No such thing as the real world in art, of course. . . . But to have created a comprehensive and coherent and recognizable whole—that's the achievement. A humane and magnanimous idea—that's *you*."

Galsworthy directed that the prize money of about £9,000 was to become a Trust Fund for the P.E.N. For all his tiredness, he and Ada devoted themselves to answering—by hand, of course—every letter of congratulation. And Galsworthy himself settled down to the composition of the address he would deliver in Stockholm when he should go there the following month to receive his honour from the Swedish king.

"To hale into the field of sight our literary pasts, that is a task—or, shall we say, a pleasure—from which the modest recoil," he began, seated in his study at Bury, pad on knee, J nib poised and bottle of ink near the dog sleeping at his feet. He wrote laboriously, but with determination, calling up from his memory the long story of his life of writing.

XXV

Two years earlier Galsworthy had been irrationally troubled by a small persistent growth, a mere spot, on the right side of his nose. He refused, however, to consult a doctor about it, and during that winter, spent in America, it cleared away, and he seemed once more in good health. During the following summer, however, he was thrown one day from his horse at Bury—possibly, his nephew later thought, because his bodily control was already slightly failing, though none suspected anything of the kind at the time. At the beginning of August he had an old Oxford friend and his wife to stay for the weekend and during dinner Galsworthy was suddenly seized with an attack of stuttering; later, in his bedroom, he had a second, longer attack. At about this time, too, the spot reappeared on the side of his nose and worried him so much that he started to turn his head away when he met anybody, to shun well-lit rooms and at last to try to avoid meeting anyone at all other than his family. He still refused to consult a doctor, but at last Rudo managed to get one to him by a stratagem. The doctor diagnosed the spot as a small rodent ulcer, curable by radium treatment. He therefore submitted to the treatment throughout that winter and into the following spring, except for a rather shorter break than usual, which he and Ada again took at Biarritz. The ulcer, as the doctor had predicted, cleared away but the state of depression into which it had plunged him persisted and the growing desire to hide from all company save his own. This was the mood in which he was writing Over the River in the summer of 1932. At that time he had his third attack of stuttering, so severe as to amount to temporary speechlessness, in his bedroom at Hampstead. It did not prevent his taking Ada away to Italy for a holiday. He continued, too, to drive with her to Newmarket for race meetings and, when at Bury, to take his regular exercise on horseback; but Rudo began to worry because he noticed that his uncle seemed to be dragging one leg slightly. He also consented for the first time in his life to use a mounting block. It is his nephew's opinion that by then he well knew that something was gravely wrong with his health—perhaps even that he was not far from death—but that he deliberately concealed any sign that he could and obstinately refused to consult a doctor because he did not wish Ada to be worried. He hoped that he would be able to die in his own home, as old Jolyon had done, without any previous medical fuss that could only plunge her into anxiety before there was any need to distress her. In fact, although Rudo and Vi both noticed symptoms in their uncle which alarmed them, Ada noticed nothing. In the autumn of 1932, for example, they saw that he could no longer control a billiards cue effectively. They deliberately left him easy shots, but he nevertheless often missed them. Ada laughed at his clumsiness, which she would certainly not have done, Rudo says, had she even suspected that he was ill. His desire to shield her from anxiety as long as he could was strengthened by the knowledge that she herself was forming a cataract on one of her eyes and was threatened towards the end of her life eventually with near blindness. That this might happen to her and he not be there to look after her, was, Rudo is sure, his uncle's gravest, almost despairing anxiety, something he could scarcely bear to contemplate.

On November 11, the day after he had heard of his Nobel Prize, he was riding a new mare, when it shied at a shining plough. Galsworthy came off on his back. When everybody rushed from the house, with the riderless horse careering about, he picked himself up, declaring that he was perfectly all right. But now even Ada began to realize that there was something amiss. "He looks *anything* but right," she wrote next day to his sister, Mabel Reynolds.

He shut himself away in his room at Bury, and continued laboriously to compose his address for Stockholm. "From what point in my past shall I start?" he wrote. "From a railway station—a railway bookstall—a voice murmuring: 'You are just the person to write, why don't you?' A startled ear, a startled voice. 'I?' Thus began the career of which you are about to glean the echoes. To me the Gare du Nord in Paris will always be haloed by that soft incitement uttered thirty-seven years ago."

When he was not writing his speech, he continued to ride over the downs behind Bury House, though not so frequently as before nor for such long periods. Then he and Ada were also busily occupied with answering the flow of letters congratulating him on his Nobel Prize. By thus filling his days, he produced a semblance of normality, but he could no longer disguise from anyone in the house that he was ill though he steadfastly refused again to see a doctor. When pressed he simply retired into his study and continued to con over his life in his Nobel speech: "In 1920, possessed by the desire to prevent anyone else from reading that dreadful little book [his first published book, the collection of nine stories bound up under the title, *From the Four Winds*] I wrote to its publisher. He had twenty copies left. Since they had no value he parted from them with I know not what alacrity. Tempted three years later by my bibliographer I sold them to the firm of which he was a member for a hundred pounds. In the boom which followed they fetched perhaps two thousand pounds. Twenty copies of my first, worst book fetched one hundred pounds apiece. Dear God, is there anything more absurd than the value of first editions? They soar, and they decline, the larks greet them in the blue and the robins bury them under leaves. . . ."

He was due to attend a P.E.N. meeting in Paris on November 23, but even he had to admit that he could not go. He was running a slight temperature and he accepted this as sufficient reason for cancelling the journey, though still declaring there was nothing of any importance wrong with him and still refusing to see a doctor.

Rudo, desperately worried at his gaunt appearance and failing clarity of speech, drafted a letter to the Nobel Committee saying that Galsworthy would not be able to travel to Stockholm to receive his prize in person. But his uncle would not on any account have it posted. Certainly he would go to Stockholm and deliver his speech; he went back into his room to continue writing it. Into it he was putting his mature reflections on the books he had written, why he had come to write them in the way that he did and how clearly he saw their deficiencies as well as their possible merits. He recalled how he began writing "in a life marked private in every corner". He dealt with the ferment of spirit and the shimmering revolt that led to *The Man of Property* and the books that followed it in the same satiric mood. He considered the novels he had written about the problems of penury: "The novelist soon loses the power of expressing his instant sympathies. The moment his name is known, the ink he uses becomes thick and clotted. I regret more than anything that I am barred—by temperament, habits of life, possessions—from the complete flow of sympathy. . . ." He considered his reputation for having set down enduring pictures of English life: "If my pictures of life have any quality of endurance, if they have any seeming truth, those pictures will be found in the long run to have been painted by one who has loved England, but never been part and parcel of the England he has loved. No novelist, playwright, writer of stories, essays and poems, has ever before so well succeeded in concealing his essence. I have made a sort of world with my pen, but has it any resemblance to the world we live in, either in England or anywhere else?" He sat in his room, musing over this question, at the end of his writing life, preparing the speech with which he would receive the outstanding literary honour. Had he told the truth about humanity, let alone about England, "It would be as true to judge France by the pictures of Maupassant," he slowly added, "or Russia by the pen pictures of Turgeniev, as to judge England by my pen pictures. We have all three been exiles all our days...."

His musings were broken by the growing insistence of his family that he must see a doctor. At last he consented to have the local man in. The doctor said that he must have a thorough examination in a clinic. But at this he immediately jibbed. He kept muttering to Vi that once you get into the hands of the doctors you never get out. He glared at the local man and told him, "You're a *detective*." Then he returned to his room, to finish writing his speech: "Why should one write: still more, why should one go on writing? To die in harness? Each writer can only answer for himself, today, tomorrow, or at some conscience-stricken date to come. It all depends on what of sentience and curiosity is left in us. Each spell or spurt of work carries within an increasing inclination to stop writing; and then, the tide runs up again. . . .

"We do not know what is coming to the civilization in which we still play our parts. . . . The surface indications are such as may bewilder newspaper prophets and whatever God there may be in the sky. But there is one constant element— human nature. The tides and currents of human feeling and of human conduct change with a speed which may best be compared with that of glaciers, or even of the mountains where those glaciers form. I would dare hazard the opinion that the field of life before us writers, twenty years hence, will, save for the colour of the grass, be practically what it is today. The present is still fettered to the past, the future to the present. . . . I am not afraid of the vanishing of civilization. I am more afraid of that moment when I shall have said all I have to say, and must just wait till Life slips behind me, says, 'Time, sir,' and I answer, 'You have been long in coming. Here is my pen—the ink in it is dry. Take it and give it to some other who will serve you better.' "

The speech was done. On Saturday, December 3, he tried to rehearse it and found he could not deliver it without stumbling. He had come downstairs unshaven that morning because he could no longer control the cut-throat razor he had always used; Vi drove him into Littlehampton to get a shave. That night, looking grim and pale, he admitted to Rudo that he was not well enough to travel to Stockholm. His nephew dispatched the necessary telegrams, a first few inquiries began to come in from newspapers, and Galsworthy retired to his bedroom, where he lay trying to read, but unable to concentrate, throwing aside one book after another.

He still resolutely refused to undergo a general examination. By now, however, Ada agreed with Rudo that it had become essential. Rudo therefore got into touch with a London specialist who was a friend of Galsworthy and he lured him to London on the pretext of wanting to see him about a portrait. When the specialist saw him, he declared that an immediate and thorough medical examination was imperative. It was now no longer possible for him even to attempt to maintain the pretence of nothing much being wrong in order not to alarm Ada. She was already deeply alarmed. Next day, therefore, Rudo tackled him and he reluctantly consented to undergo an examination which would last for two days in a London nursing home. It is Rudo's belief that Galsworthy never forgave him for forcing this examination upon him. They were all four driven to London in the Austin, a drive which Rudo counts his worst experience. Galsworthy sat throughout in silence, looking as though he had already received a death sentence and were on the way to execution. They left him sitting alone in the middle of a reception room at the nursing home in Park Lane, "obviously suffering dreadfully". While in the nursing home he took many hours to write, with Ada's help, an inscription on the title page of one of his books to present to the specialist. It was his last piece of consecutive writing.

The examination discovered nothing worse than four badly abscessed teeth, a small duodenal ulcer, poor blood-count, a silting-up of blood vessels in and around the brain; the verdict was that Galsworthy was suffering from non-pernicious anaemia, and there was definitely no growth or tumour. This news was taken to Grove Lodge, where he had taken refuge, happy to be once more among his own things but too weak to attempt the return journey to Sussex. He was having difficulty again with his speech and with movement of his limbs. There was something in particular that was worrying him, though for a time none of them could discover what it was; eventually Vi understood that he was anxious lest the servants at Bury should not get their Christmas gift of £5 each. She at once went to Bury to take them the money and he seemed comforted. But next day he was faced with the problem of endorsing the cheque for the Nobel Prize payment, which was brought to him by a man from Hambros Bank. He at last accomplished this, and Rudo took the cheque to Lloyds Bank for the P.E.N. Club.

Four days before Christmas the abscessed teeth were extracted and he made something of a recovery, even instructing that his bed was to be turned with the sun, to keep his head in sunlight; it was a particularly bright period of winter that year. But on Christmas Day his speech began to fail again and deterioration set in. He could understand what was being said and his distress at not being able to communicate was marked. Rudo noted in his diary an example of the kind of broken speech to which he was reduced: "J.G. suddenly: 'Brigbragen . . . a . . . abrigen . . . brabrigen.' R: 'Is it something you want?' 'Yes.' 'The brushes?' 'No.' 'The mirror?' 'Yes.' This is all the consecutive speech possible."

More specialists were called in and after further examination they still gave the opinion that there was no growth in the head.

Throughout December 30 Galsworthy was trying to communicate something special, and Rudo to find out what it was: " 'Is it about money?' 'No.' 'Is it about business?' 'No.' 'Is it about Auntie?' 'Yes.' " But he could get no further. He suddenly climbed out of bed and walked up and down in great agitation, mumbling something that sounded like, ". . . jump . . . a spring." Then he seized Rudo's hand and shook it hard three times, saying, "Good-bye, good-bye, good-bye." Later Ada managed to calm him down. He sat for a while by the fire, with her kneeling by his chair. That night Rudo and Vi kept vigil outside his door until 3.45 a.m., but he seemed to be sleeping.

There followed two days of great distress. He tried to say something but could not. He kept scribbling incomprehensible messages on a pad of paper, but the only two legible phrases were meaningless: "Tax: two years, I've enjoyed too pleasant circumstances . . . a year . . . one draft" and "children, how do it not here with our home". The only thing that interested him was an evening newspaper account of a test match; the only thing that seemed to comfort him was for Ada to play him sonatas after tea, accompanied by Rudo on the flute. She did eventually, however, discover that he was worried about tax payments, and managed with great difficulty to get him to sign two necessary cheques; not long afterwards he signed a power of attorney for her.

It was during these early days of the New Year that the surgeons began to fear the presence of a brain tumour. He had recovered a little lucidity and admitted to some symptoms, such as headaches at night, of which previously he had told nobody; it is Rudo's opinion that he deliberately tried to suppress some of the symptoms in order to deceive the surgeons, and thus, as he presumably thought, render less alarming the report they would make to Ada. More doctors were called in —by the end he had been seen by ten. They asked for an X-ray examination of the head, the preparations for which greatly upset Galsworthy and which in the event showed nothing. But now the diagnosis was definitely a tumour. Ada, who was beginning to grow hysterical outside the sickroom (though, in his presence, her cheerfulness and pretence of normality never for a moment failed), declared that he would not consent to an operation. Galsworthy himself had relapsed into non-communication and bodily clumsiness; he accidentally knocked over an azalea in a pot, and this unduly disturbed and fretted him. He "looks and looks and looks with great hollow eyes and drawn face," noted Rudo in his diary, "afraid he knows as much as we and can't say a word. Looking, staring, into . . . what? Something vastly terrifying or hopeless, that is certain." He had once told Rudo that he would give anything to believe that he would meet Ada in a future life; but could not. He was relapsing into semi-consciousness. The surgeons, after further examination, gave their opinion that not only was there a growth in the brain, but it was secondary to one lower down, which could not be located; this excluded any question of operation. They thought the end would be only weeks distant. Ada was most desperately distressed but continued to keep up bravely in the sickroom, talking cheerfully to him and, in the evenings, joining with Rudo in their piano and flute duets, which seemed most to please him. Outside the door ironic or macabre little incidents were happening. The Nobel Prize gold medal was delivered to the house, together with an illuminated scroll. His sister, Mabel Reynolds, in deep distress but quite unable to change her zest for new enthusiasms, came round to recommend earnestly that they should try homeopathy. A police sergeant knocked at the door; a man whom Galsworthy had helped had got into trouble again down at Southampton, and he must attend the court there, to speak for him. The police sergeant, told that he was too ill, went away. Next day he was back; he would require, please, a doctor's certificate that the patient was not in fit condition to travel to South-ampton to give evidence. Upstairs, in a bed that was slightly turned every now and then to keep his head in the winter sunlight, the patient lay most of the time in coma and was beginning to suffer slight heart attacks. There was a moment of lucidity when Vi thought she had managed to get through to him the assurance that all would be well with Ada. But the doctors were saying that nothing further could be done.

The news of his illness now became public in the Press. There was at once a constant flow of callers at the door with flowers, an incessant stream of inquiries. The King and Queen, who were at Sandringham, sent for news. The Prime Minister telephoned. In every post there were letters from strangers which Rudo had to try to keep from Ada, since they described miraculous recoveries of other people in circumstances that could not possibly fit Galsworthy's case. But she by now was clutching at any hope and tending to talk wildly. Indeed, at almost the last moment she called in another doctor who thought there was a remote possibility of the disease's being a very rare form of anaemia; he took blood samples to analyse,

On January 29 the patient's temperature started to rise above 100 degrees. Ada had been praying that, if he had to die, it should be when the sun was shining. But next day it be-came so foggy that they had to shut the bedroom window; Rudo noted almost automatically that there was a robin sing-ing outside. During the day there came a letter from the last-called doctor reporting on the blood samples; the letter removed the last hope, for the tests showed no trace of anaemia. That day and the following night, Galsworthy's deep distress could be alleviated only by morphia. He died at a quarter past nine next morning. When they drew back the curtains, the sun was shining.

Before the body was removed from Grove Lodge to be cremated, Rudo made three drawings of his uncle's head as it rested in death. He worked throughout the night in order not to disturb Ada, and noted that the aspect of the head gradually changed and that by the end of the second night "the whole figure had altered to the likeness of some mediaeval saint in his last repose".

The Authors' Society put forward a request that his ashes should be buried in Westminster Abbey, but to this the Dean of Westminster would not consent. He did, however, permit a Memorial Service in the Abbey, to which all the distinguished world went, as well as many ordinary people whose only connection with Galsworthy was that they had read and loved his novels.

One of the poems he had written at Bury House in Sussex, on a single piece of notepaper, was an instruction to "Scatter my Ashes! Let them be free to the air. . . . Let them be grey in the dawn, Bright if the noontime be bright, And when night's curtain is drawn Starry and dark with the night. . . ."

The instruction was carried out on a spring day at the end of March 1933. His ashes were scattered on the top of Bury Hill, on the turf across which he used to ride every day that he lived in the house below and from which the view reaches across beechwoods to a distant sight of the sea.

INDEX